# A CAREER GUIDE FOR BLACK MALE STUDENT-ATHLETES:

## AN ALTERNATIVE TO THE PROS

CHARLES RICHBURG, ED.D.

# A CAREER GUIDE FOR BLACK MALE STUDENT-ATHLETES:

## AN ALTERNATIVE TO THE PROS

### CHARLES RICHBURG, ED.D.

African American Images

Chicago, Illinois

# Praise for the Author of a Career Guide for Black Male Student-Athletes

As a dear, longtime friend of Dr. Charles Richburg, I am delighted to see him achieve yet another one of his goals along his journey. I have been a part of Dr. Richburg's life for over 25 years. He has inspired and helped me to get my life back on track. Several years ago, I followed him to earn my baccalaureate and master's degrees. Furthermore, Dr. Richburg was my supervisor during my introduction to the noWt-for-profit arena in Westchester County, New York.

During his academic journey, I distinctly remember the stories he would share about being an avid basketball player in his heyday and would see the joy in his eyes when he reminisced about those days. He shared the trials and tribulations of growing up as Black youth in the south and what sports meant to him, both then and now. It is no surprise that "Doc," as he is affectionately known by those of us closest to him, chose to write about a subject that he is so passionate about.

After reading his manuscript, I was drawn in by both the "voice" and writing style that he displays. If I were a struggling student-athlete and I came across this book, I would definitely be "forced" to do some introspection, which in my opinion, is one of Doc's goals and purposes for writing this book. Delving a little further into the manuscript and knowing his background, this book is sure to serve as a road map for any young person as well as adults with children to help them to "find their way" and successfully start and stay on their path to academic and life success as they begin the process of identifying their life goal(s) paths. Dr. Richburg's life experience as well as academic background, coupled with his expertise on this subject, is sure to be thought-provoking, inspiring and a "road map and blueprint" for life!

KEVIN D. MCGILL, MS, ADJUNCT PROFESSOR, STATE UNIVERSITY OF
NEW YORK (SUN.Y),
OWNER AND MEDIA PRODUCTIONS COORDINATOR, KEVSTERVISION.COM

# DEDICATION

First and foremost, to the God who is known by many names I give thanks for all that I have! In memory of my parents, the late Charles "*Big Lefty*" Richburg, Jr. and Mozella Richburg. To my wife Judith, my goddaughter Essence, sisters Bobbie and Janet Fitten, my brother Johnnie, my beloved family and to the next generations of my nephews and nieces this book is for you.

Finally, to the Black male student-athletes whose path to success has been cluttered with a plethora of obstacles and yet their desire to succeed may be somewhat unfathomable at this point on their life's journey. May some of the words, ideas, and passion expressed here be useful in some way to them. To all my young brothers, I salute you all!

# TABLE OF CONTENTS

# ACKNOWLEDGMENTS

To name all of those who have aided in the development of this book would require multiple pages and even that would be insufficient. However, I would like to acknowledge some of the contributors. First is my wife whose encouragement and patience were vital to my continuing when I did not feel like working, she pushed and encouraged me, for that I am grateful. To my dear late friend brother Abdul-Hasib Matin, an accomplished writer, author, and writing instructor who spent many hours reviewing and making suggestions during the book's development; he was invaluable.

I am eternally grateful to Dr. Jawanza Kunjufu and his publishing company African American Images, Inc., located in Chicago, Illinois, for their willingness to provide all the necessary guidance to a first-time book author like myself. And to the many unnamed others whose encouragement and insights all contributed to the development of this book. It is hoped that my work will serve as an example for Black male student-athletes and teach them all the value of sharing of one's self! There have been so many who have contributed to my knowledge and experience gained during my 30 plus years of serving as an advocate for the less fortunate among us, irrespective of the area of need. To my editor, Ms. Mary Lewis, whose tireless efforts and patience and skills aided my development as a first-time author. I could not have done it without her!

# FOREWORD

Although this book is targeted for Black male athletes it is also good for non-athletes, and others interested in exploring different ways of redefining purpose, perspective, and progress. *A Career Guide for Black Male Student-Athletes: An Alternative to the Pros* allows the reader to walk in the steps of a student-athlete replete with ups and downs not uncommon for teens in an urban setting. What is unsuspecting is the author's candor and transparency as he shares his life struggles during the civil rights era, and then coming of age during the 1960s. But with help from those he encounters, and lessons learned he emerges to tell his story in hopes of helping others avoid the pitfalls he encountered. Dr. C's resiliency and transparency allow us to have a brief glimpse of the soul of a black man unabashedly sharing his struggles and successes of his life that against all odds he transitions from the playground to the boardroom. What was it that spurred him to complete the winning play?

Dr. C is the son of Big Lefty, a pitcher on the Negro Leagues' Atlanta Black Crackers team, and the grandson of a Buffalo Soldier. It is a combination of the love of the basketball game and the love of service that stirred in Dr. C the promise to teach and counsel those like him, to remember that their victories as athletes are a precursor to a productive life. This guide is not a self-help book or a fairy tale of false promises. Within these pages you will find strategies and principles to guide you in your decision making, fundamental practices to live by, and to contribute to family and community. Travel through the pages with Dr. C, read and then read again to get understanding, then, take the shot!

*JUDITH M. RICHBURG, MPA*

# INTRODUCTION

## My Story

Before ever putting pen to paper and fingers on the keyboard, I wondered if I had enough material to fill the pages of the type of book I wanted to write and share with all of my readers, especially my target audience—Black male student-athletes and their supporters, including their counselors, academic advisors, and family members.

A dear friend of 40+ years, the late Abdul Matin, was an accomplished author with several publications throughout the nation as well as in several foreign countries. He gave me excellent advice regarding writing this, my first book, because he knew much of my life's story—the good, bad, and the ugly. He said, "Charlie, just start writing, brother."

As a former student-athlete and because of my strong identification with Black male student-athletes who were never able to fully capitalize on their skills and talent, I realized the importance of sharing how this book was first conceived. I realized that I should tell a portion of my story and how sharing my story could hopefully be the archway through which I could connect with those young brothers who hope to become successful pros after completing the academic portion of their life's journey. As the book's title suggest, there are many pathways to becoming a professional, not only a professional athlete but a professional in a plethora of industries. More on this later.

As a high school basketball player in the mid- to late 1960s with considerable talent according to many, there were times I thought about and wondered if I was good enough to make the pros one day. I was a high school sophomore in 1965, attending Washington Senior High School in Pensacola, Florida. I played on the junior varsity team for a brief period and was elevated to the varsity squad almost immediately. This was unusual; in those days, sophomores (10th graders) could only play on the junior varsity team. Our varsity team was comprised of several good and a couple of great players. During this period in the country's history, in the early to mid-1960s, public schools in Pensacola and in many other areas in the South were racially segregated. Blacks attended their schools and the Caucasians attended theirs. Since segregation was all I knew at the time I just accepted it as a way of life, a way of life that I did not agree with. Although I knew innately that I had to be careful with what and who I asked questions about why things were the way they were.

One specific day is still as etched in my mind more than 50 years later as if it happened yesterday. I can still see my father's face when I asked him why we had to walk into the front door of the public transportation bus, place our money in the coin collector, and get off the bus and walk to the back door of the bus and only be allowed to sit in the rear and smallest section of the bus labeled: Colored Only. God forbid if a White person wanted to sit in the "colored" section of the bus; they would be looked at as being strange for wanting to sit with "those people." My dad never answered me verbally; however, the look of sadness and powerlessness in his eyes provided me with the answer. Still, dad knew that law was simply wrong! Yet I somehow knew instinctively that to attempt to break or violate any of the laws of segregation could not only bring trouble for me and our family it could lead to a fatality if one was not careful. My dad was a true alpha male and yet the lesson I learned over the years from his ability to restrain himself when confronted with injustices of this nature was what courage and sacrifice really meant. You see, dad made the choice many times to take the way of peace, rather being right!

Here is an example of the result of one of my exploratory adventures. Sometimes my mother would send me downtown in Pensacola to pay bills, and one day I decided to take the bold step of stopping and drinking from the "Whites Only" water fountain. Of course, I had to make sure that I was not seen by anyone Black or White. To my amazement the water tasted the same as it did everywhere else I had drank from, including at home. I remember thinking, what is the big deal, the water tastes the same. Since the public drinking fountains were in such close proximity to the restrooms, I figured I would continue my exploration to see if I could distinguish the differences in the restrooms as well. There was none. If a White person saw me drinking from or entering or exiting the Whites Only facilities, especially a White man, he'd probably say to me as many did during those days, "Hey boy," or "Hey, nigger, y'all's bathroom is out back." This actually happened to me. Once a White man saw me preparing to enter the Whites Only men's room and yelled. "Hey nigger, y'all's bathroom is over there," pointing as he spoke. Such were the experiences of my first 15.5 years of being born and living in the Deep South. During the summer of 1967, I moved to New York City to rejoin my mother who had moved to New York City to take a job as a domestic worker.

During the year that Mom and I were separated I lived with Mom's sisters, my two favorite aunts Gracie and Julia. We had always been a close family. When I was born in 1950, I was the only baby and much of the attention was given to me. The biggest change that took place in my life happened on June 30, 1966 and would forever change my life's trajectory. On June 30, 1966, my father died suddenly of a heart attack at the age of 50! I have always believed and I still do, the most important time that a boy needs his father is between the ages of 16-21. This need is especially relevant for Black boys. I was 16 when dad passed.

A few months later mom and I moved from New York City to Westchester County, New York. In September 1967 I enrolled as a high school junior in New Rochelle High School. As stated earlier, I attended segregated schools from the 1st to the 10th grade before moving to New York.

What made my enrollment in New Rochelle High School extraordinary was that this was my first time ever sitting in a classroom with classmates and teachers who did not look like me! Although I did not know what to expect, I was prepared and quite frankly looking forward to interacting with my new classmates and teachers.

My transition was surprisingly easy. One contributing factor to the easy transition stemmed I believe from my status as a star basketball player on the school's varsity basketball team. Before ever setting foot on the campus the sports editor for the local newspaper conducted research related to my basketball prowess at my former high school in Pensacola and concluded that I would be the key player to help our school to finally get over "the hump" when it came to defeating our two biggest rivals.

Both schools were perennial powers in the region when it came to boys' basketball. As a matter of fact, to this very day Mount Vernon High School has had more of their former players enter the National Basketball Association (NBA) than all other high schools in Westchester County combined. Readers may recognize former NBA players like Gus and Ray Williams, the McCray brothers Scooter and Rodney, and Earl Tatum, to name a few.

Prior to my arrival on the NRHS campus, most coaches, fans, and interested parties such as the neighborhood gamblers commonly known as "numbers bankers and runners" made bets on the area's high school basketball games. It was during those years 1967–68 that I began to capitalize on opportunities to make some quick money. Mr. Joe W., a big-time numbers banker in the region, would always ask how many points I thought we could win by. My reply was always the same: "How many do you need us to win or lose by?" Of course, after each game I was given an envelope that contained anywhere from $100.00 to $250.00. In the mid- to late 1960s the value of the dollar during those days was a nice bit of pocket change for a 17-year-old to have with no visible means of income. Because of that "hustle" I was able to help mom with our bills. In years to come when I look back on those days, I am not proud of what I did to fix games. For me it was simply a survival tool, or so I thought at the time. Unfortunately, I only played on the team during my junior year. The following school year saw the return of all the key players from the team that won 17 of 21 games the previous season.

Although my game improved steadily, I also began to using drugs to get high, initially recreationally. At some point getting high became more important than focusing on basketball and class attendance although I had several scholarships offers from several basketball powers, such as Villanova University, the University of Iowa, Iowa State University, and Memphis State University, to name a few. With no real father figure in my life, I didn't have the right type of guidance or more importantly I did not seek out the proper guidance needed at the time to help me understand that the decisions made between the ages of 16 to21 are generally the most critical period in a boy's life, especially among Black boys like me.

As I stated previously my father died when I was 16. Although Mom was the best mother a guy could have, she was not able to do the job of mother and father. God knows she tried, and I have loved her for that every day of my life! I began gravitating toward the guys in the street whom I thought of as living the life that I admired. You know the types, the ones with the nice cars and clothes, pockets full of cash, and all the girls. These guys never punched a time clock and surely did not work for "the man." Little did I know at that time that the "real cool guys" were those who took care of their families, spent quality time with their children, had careers in various industries, and never had to worry about avoiding law enforcement because for the most part they lived honorable lives. As a result of being attracted to the guys on the street corners commonly known as "hustlers," these guys eventually became my mentors and drug connections.

There was only one guy, a drug connection of mine who one night pulled me to the side as I went to make a purchase of what by this time had become a daily habit of heroin use, he said the following: "Hey Charlie, you have some real talent and you're smart in school too unlike a lot of these dudes, you have something going for yourself. He continued by saying that most of these guys are never going to be anything but what they are right now, drug addicts, alcoholics, and going in and out of jail. But you, you really have something that can take you away from this and you can be somebody!" Unfortunately for me, I paid no attention to what he said, all I wanted was to purchase my drugs and get high. Sadly, that is all that mattered during those times.

Therefore, despite the scholarship offers for a "full ride" to some of the best colleges and universities in the country, 17 days after my 19th birthday, I found myself in a long-term residential drug treatment program known as a therapeutic community. I spent the next 18–24 months in a place called The Renaissance Project. While many of my peers were beginning their post-high school careers attending some college or university, here I was in a TC. However, while there in the TC I learned many valuable life lessons, some of which I continue to practice and respect to this very day.

At some point as I came closer to completing my drug treatment in the TC, I began to think more seriously about my basketball talent and maybe getting a second chance of sorts. However, somewhere along the way, I decided I wanted to be a counselor and help people like me who had the same problems I had. It soon became apparent that the people who ran the program, they also thought that I could be an effective drug counselor. While wrapping up my treatment I was approached by the leadership and offered an opportunity to begin my paid training as a staff trainee.

Although I had not played basketball competitively for almost two years, I continued playing with guys in the treatment center who after a few months of being alcohol/drug free, eating and resting properly provided good competition. A few of the players were former American Basketball Association (ABA) pros. Two former ABA players stood out and both still "had game" in spite of their involvement with alcohol and drugs just as I did. To avoid violating their anonymity I'll use only their first names and last initials. Dexter W. and Wally J. were all-star caliber players during their ABA days, and I remember competing against them and realizing that not only could I hold my own, my "basketball fires" seemed to be reignited and the dream of possibly playing at the Division I level and beyond was once again awakened. However, by this time my heart was set on being a drug counselor. Therefore, I invested my energy and focused on learning my craft as a drug counselor. I recall one specific incident that piqued my interest again in playing Division I basketball. The program where I began my training as a drug counselor had a facility in lower Westchester County about 10 miles outside of New York City. This was a transitional facility for program participants who had completed the residential portion of their treatment and were being phased back into mainstream society after 12–18 months. The term "magic mountain" was coined because of the success the program had with many of its former residents, including me. Several of them re-entered the workforce and returned to college to earn their degrees which they had started before alcohol and drugs became a permanent fixture in their lives.

During the summer of 1972 while residing in the Phase-Out House I was told that I had a visitor. Upon entering the living quarters of the house, I met a man who introduced himself as the assistant men's basketball coach for Memphis State University (known today as the University of Memphis). The assistant coach was a Black man of medium build and height and did not strike me as a former basketball player at all. After introducing himself he went right to the reason for his visit. He stated that he was prepared to offer me a full scholarship to attend MSU and play for their team. I was overwhelmed and flattered by his offer. However, there was a caveat: I had to be willing to leave with him the next morning. Since my dad had died six years prior, I thought to myself what advice would dad have given had he been here? Since both the executive director and program director were on the premises, I consulted with them on what I should do. Both had been like a father figure, and they simply replied, "Charlie, that is totally your call." Although neither of them had a background in athletics, they were as supportive as they could be based on their knowledge, or lack thereof. I informed the coach that I would need more time and understood that he too had a schedule to keep. In the end, I decided to pass on his offer. Besides, I did not want to leave Mom alone again since I had been in treatment for the past 24 months and was seeing her only on weekend visits.

Although I declined the offer to attend MSU, I also realized that second chances are possible. Therefore, if you are one who has had some missteps in your early life, I encourage you to not give up on your dream. I truly believe and have experienced what happens when one does the right things, the right things will happen!

Another factor that may have influenced my decision had to do with the time we lived in. During those days the racial and social turmoil that existed throughout the United States was intense and leaving the New York City area to live in the Deep South was a somewhat frightening proposition, in spite of the fact that I moved from the segregated South in Pensacola, only a few short years prior. Memphis and the surrounding region were a hotbed of racial tensions, protest marches, etc., and I was not sure if I could make the necessary adjustments. One thing I did know was that good athletes no matter their racial composition were treated differently and better than non-athletic Black boys and men attending college during those years. In the South they love or appear to love their sports figures at all levels, high school, college, and pros, and still do to this very day.

Over the years I have often thought about what might have been had I made the decision to accept the offer to attend and play for Memphis State University. Of course, over the next few years I continued to follow men's basketball college and pro. In the 1973 NCAA Men's Basketball Championship game the Memphis State University Tigers lost to legendary Coach John Wooden and the UCLA Bruins by a score of 87–66. I remember thinking on several occasions over the years, that I had an opportunity to be a starting small forward on that MSU team and wondered if I could have made a difference in the outcome of that game. One of life's greatest lessons I learned and hold on to this very day all these years later is, that Time Is a Gift, not a Threat!

Over the next few years there were several other opportunities to play at the collegiate and semi-pro levels; however, my passion for continuing to play had begun to dissipate. By now I was nearing my 25th birthday and though I played serious pickup ball with guys who had been Division I and former pro players, my passion for playing was no longer there. What remained was my developing career as a counselor.

## What happens to many Black male student-athletes?

Unless and until a concentrated effort is made by the Black male student-athletes themselves, along with genuine efforts by those in academic and athletic leadership at various academic institutions throughout America, the trend of athletes not completing their education and earning their degrees, will produce dismal outcomes at best. Although there have been and continue to be a plethora of studies on why the Black male student-athlete population continues to lag so far behind the general population when it comes to earning their degrees, none in the author's view have captured the essence of the problems better than Shaun R. Harper, PhD. At the time of this writing Dr. Harper served as executive director of the Center for the Study of Race and Equity in Education at the University of Pennsylvania's Graduate School of Education.

Dr. Harper contends that revenue-generating colleges and universities continue to profit at a rate of tens or in some cases hundreds of millions of dollars annually across a broad spectrum of collegiate athletics. In the meantime, the "student" part of student-athletes gets left behind. Dismal though the situation appears to be, it is not irreversible. In a report titled: *Black Male Student-Athletes and Racial Inequities in the National Collegiate Athletic Association (NCAA) Division I Revenue-Generating College Sports,* Dr. Harper, along with colleagues Collin D. William Jr., and Horatio W. Blackman, provided in my opinion, an excellent road map for addressing the dismal graduation rates for Blacks in general and Black male student-athletes in particular. Although the report focused on the top seven NCAA Division I revenue-generating universities in major sport conferences, Black male student-athletes in lower ranking colleges and universities all face similar plights generally speaking.

The leaders in the various institutions of higher learning, such as college and university presidents, trustees, faculty members, and athletic administrators, must be motivated to create and enforce policies, demand transparency, and establish a system for collecting raw data from the athletic leadership to help ensure ample support staff are in place to demand more of their Black male student-athletes than their performance in their particular sport(s). For example, by encouraging or requiring Black male student-athletes to become more active in campus-wide academic activities, and by encouraging Black male student-athletes to consider immersing themselves in activities outside of athletics, this could be a gateway to accessing more academic support from fellow students as well as their instructors. As the old adage states: "When the student is ready, the teacher will appear." This appearance can come in a variety of ways, only if the student is ready.

Many of today's Black male student-athletes are isolated the minute they set foot on campus. For example, they are provided with separate living quarters reserved exclusively for the student-athletes, aka "jocks." The message many of the student-athletes receive is that they are a separate or "privileged" student because of their athletic prowess. Admittedly, the life of the student-athlete is not without its challenges. For example, the typical student-athlete must contend with attending classes, and when it comes to finding time to study, practice can often occur in the early morning hours on into the evening hours and they also must squeeze in time to study and practice for upcoming games. Moreover, they must contend with travel schedules which at times can interfere with class attendance and which requires studying while on the road. Establishing or attempting to establish and maintain a social life is indeed a challenge for the most dedicated student-athlete. When it comes to Black male student-athletes, isolation and a sense of "privilege," compounded by the challenge of college-level academics make for a disconnect when we consider the statistics on their graduation rates.

Statistically speaking, research confirms that most Black male student-athletes tend to drop-out of college between their sophomore and senior years. I researched the success rate of Black male student-athletes who had begun work on their bachelor's degrees. Sadly, I discovered that the number of Black men who begin their pursuit of their baccalaureate degree and never complete them ran almost parallel to the number of Black male student-athletes who also failed to earn their baccalaureate degrees. Statistically, as of this writing, only 50 percent of Black male student-athletes enrolled in seven of the major NCAA Division I sports conferences graduate within six years. Perhaps the realization sets in that they may not be receiving a call from a professional sports organization and therefore they begin developing a "what the hell attitude." The primary question that must be asked by every Black male student-athlete is: Am I an athlete who happens to be a student or am I a student who happens to be an athlete? Honestly answering this and other questions could be the make-or-break point that helps them understand why such dismal outcomes occur when it comes to Black male student-athletes graduating with their college degrees.

I sincerely believe that this pattern can and will be broken eventually. Perhaps we can begin with you if you are in one of the categories mentioned.

It is quite possible or more likely that many Black male student-athletes have dreamed of one day going pro and therefore, school is just a means to an end to the pros. This is understandable and yet the reality demands that other avenues be explored. Within the pages of this book are questions to ponder and self-assessment tools that if taken seriously have tremendous value for helping members of this group to assess exactly where they stand as it pertains to their ability to become paid professional athletes. Also within the pages of this book are opportunities for Black male student-athletes to give serious consideration to a plethora of opportunities available to them to become "pros" in many industries outside of professional sports organizations.

While reflecting on my life experiences, the one group of Black males who have always held a special place in my mind and heart are Black male student-athletes. Over the years I have worked with members of society who were faced with numerous academic, social, economic, and spiritual challenges, and I realized the need for proper guidance and caring support. As a result of my passionate concern for members of this group, at the age of 60 I decided to pursue my doctoral degree in education. I thought, perhaps those to whom I have been drawn to help the most would listen and heed the words of Dr. Richburg better than they could hear Charles Richburg.

As you read through this book, I implore you to along with Black male student-athletes to consider those who truly care about this group to provide support and counsel Whatever your role may be as professors, coaches, student support services providers, and especially family members and friends to help these young men see and realize that the universe allows one to have more than one dream! In addition, statistical data is available to help bring the picture into clear view for the many Black male student-athletes who aspire to become professional athletes.

Dear readers, please understand, it is not my intention to discourage any Black male student-athlete from pursuing what for many of them has been a dream since they were little boys. All that I am asking them to do is, consider the many opportunities available within and without the professional sports industry. Positioning themselves to have a plethora of options is based on their willingness and desire to stay and earn their degree(s)!

# Primary Purpose of This Book

At first glance you probably thought when you saw the book's title, A Career Guide for Black Male Student-Athletes: An Alternative to the Pros that this was possibly a book about becoming a professional athlete. The book was designed to remind readers that there is a plethora of ways to become a "pro." Take a moment and reflect on what being a pro really means. If you dissect the term professional or pro, I am sure you will agree that becoming a professional simply means that you have devoted the time, energy, desire, and hard work needed to be good at whatever undertaking you decide to pursue. This also means that as a pro, your level of skills, experience, and reputation should or does earn you an income to be proud of. To be sure, we need to have a good working definition of the term professional or pro. Here is one definition of professional: "Relating to a job that requires special education, training, or skill" (www.merriam-webster.com/dictionary/professional).

However, this definition would be incomplete without including the term, "passion." Interestingly, if you notice, none of the many dictionaries use terms like the National Basketball Association (NBA), National Football League (NFL), Major League Baseball (MLB), etc., to define "professional." Yet, the need for special education, training, skill, and passion are the prerequisites for becoming a pro in any industry or field. I sincerely hope that when you have finished reading this book, perhaps you will have a better or different understanding of the many ways it means to be a "pro."

When I realized the real value and peace that can be found when one decides to look deep within one's self, I found that one day I could pursue my long-held passion of reaching out to Black male student-athletes to inform or remind them that they too can be a pro. I realized several years ago that my passion was to continue working with and guiding as many Black male student-athletes as I could to turn pro someday. I wanted to help this group by using my 30+ years' experience as a general counselor, college professor, career, and entrepreneurial developmental professional. Fortunately for me, that day arrived and this book is a testament to my passion for serving others.

Moreover, my interest in this group (Black male student-athletes) was such that I returned to college at the age of 60 to earn my doctorate degree in education to better position myself to serve. My drive to complete my doctoral studies served to motivate me even more. Perhaps some are wondering why I bring this up. When we look at the path that comprises Black male student-athlete's lives, a pattern emerges, of not completing something as important as their formal education whether it is their bachelor's, master's, or doctorate degree. For many Black male student-athletes the reason for dropping out of school is quite simple. It is likely that they have yet to be contacted by a professional sports organization, which puts a damper on their aspirations and many quit school.

## How to Use This Book

To help guide readers to the best ways to use this book, is to help readers recognize that each chapter is devoted to helping Black male student-athletes and those who support them. Along those lines, most chapters end with a section called *Questions to Ponder*, which allows student-athletes to pause and consider the chapter's topic and its relevance to their outlook on their lives.

One of the most challenging portions of the book for the Black male student-athletes can be found in chapter one, the *Self-Assessment Survey for the Black Male Student-Athlete.* Since all responses to the survey are subjective, there are no right or wrong answers. The survey's primary purpose is to help each Black male student-athlete to conduct an honest self-assessment based on the inquiries provided and use that assessment to frame their outlook and plans for becoming a pro. Furthermore, I encourage you to go beyond the survey if needed and use the inquiries as a type of prolegomena for further self-discovery.

In addition, the book is designed to help Black male student-athletes realize what great opportunities they have to really explore both their academic and athletic selves. Therefore, readers are encouraged to read each chapter with the idea in mind to help themselves and other members of this group weigh what could be the most important decisions in their life.

Here is a special message to those Black male student-athletes who really feel or have evidence, such as having received contact from one or more professional sports organizations, that their chances are high of being hired by a professional sports organization when they leave school, hopefully after earning their degree. Of course, with some of the new eligibility rules approved for implementation in the near future, some athletes may choose to leave school before graduating, especially if their situation as described above is a good fit. If that turns out to be your situation, I applaud you!

However, for the vast majority of Black male student-athletes, it is imperative that they see, along with those in leadership positions in academic administration and those who counsel or otherwise provide support to these young men, that their best chance of having a fulfilling post-college life that they can be proud of, is to stay and earn their degrees. There are many, many ways to become a professional outside of playing professional sports. Research will confirm that many former Black male student-athletes who did not earn positions on any professional sports teams, have had and are having successful careers in practically every industry that exists. Hopefully, by using this book you will be awaken your awareness of the world of professions and how you can discover your place as a pro.

I pray that this book has value for you, no matter your current station in life!

# CHAPTER ONE

# The Forgotten Student: The Black Male Student-Athlete

A few years ago, I stopped in a local fast-food eatery to grab a bite to eat. While waiting in line I was reviewing my cell phone messages. With my eyes still focused on my cell phone, which often seems like a "body part" because it is always with me, I heard a familiar voice asking, "Would you like fries with that?" I looked up at the young man asking the question, and I realized that he was familiar to me. Perhaps I gave it away when I said I looked up. Keep in mind that I am 6'6" tall, so when I must look up to someone, they must be taller than 6'6". This encounter was all too familiar to me. This particular young man was one of the hundreds, perhaps thousands of young men who "had game," yet as a 21-year-old he was obviously not playing college or professional basketball and therefore probably not going to receive a call from the National Basketball Association (NBA). How did this young man's life journey take him from being a highly touted high school All-American just a few short years ago to working in McDonald's? Please understand, I am not degrading those who work in fast-food industry. Many great careers can be developed because of a start at a McDonald's or similar eateries. More importantly, this young man had begun his college career; he made it to a college campus which in and of itself is an important accomplishment for any Black male. Statistically, at this writing there are four Black females to every one Black male attending college in the United States of America.

The impetus for this book was born from my encounter with this young man. When I decided to return to college to earn my doctorate degree, I surmised from the outset that I had to identify a topic or area of interest that I was passionate enough about, so when the rigors of doctoral study began to become evident, I would be willing to continue in spite of the challenges presented academically, emotionally, financially, and spiritually. As I stated in my introduction, as a former student-athlete who had several scholarships offers and opportunities to attend college years earlier, unfortunately, when I reached my proverbial "fork in the road" I took a "left" rather than a "right turn." My left turn led me to having to make life-and-death decisions on practically a daily basis. At the age of 18 rather than going to prison for crimes I had committed to support my heroin habit, I was offered an opportunity to enter a long-term residential substance abuse program in upstate New York. It was during my 24 months in that treatment program that I realized I wanted to help, aid, and assist others who were afflicted with the same diseases of alcoholism and drug addiction that I had. It was at this point that my training as a counselor began.

If you have this book in hand perhaps you or someone you know has dreamed at one time or another of making a living playing the sport they love professionally. Over the years I have met many such young men. Although many of them made it to a college or university campus for reasons perhaps known only to them, they were not quite sure of their abilities and talents academically or athletically for that matter. The great news that this book will hopefully provide is, that there are many ways to be a "pro." Although it's only natural for many to think of themselves as having the potential to turn pro, unfortunately, many never look beyond the athletic arena.

For those in this category, why did you not make it to the table to sign that first contract? There is an old African proverb that provides the following admonition: Man Know Thy Self. Another proverb reads; One Must Seek Knowledge from the Cradle to the Grave!

## Inequities and the Status Quo

Think with me if you would about all the Black male student-athletes and street ballers you know and played with and competed against over the years, who aspired to turn pro one day. What happened to them? Go back to your middle school years. How many guys from your school or neighborhood that you played with and against did you think had the potential to be a pro athlete one day? In your view, has the situation become better or has it worsened?

In a January 24, 2014 article Shaun R. Harper, PhD, wrote the following for *The Chronicle of Higher Education*, "Black Men as College Athletes: The Real Win-Loss Record," he argues that education can be a vehicle for changing lives (Harper, 2014). Along with Dr. Harper and others, I agree wholeheartedly that too many Black male student-athletes leave school without their degrees. Although these statistical realities are disappointing, I am not intimidated by such statistical data. I knew when I researched Black male community college student-athletes as I did while in pursuit of my doctorate degree (Richburg, 2013), it could possibly help me to better understand why Black male student-athletes represented the group with the lowest graduation completion rate particularly at the baccalaureate level.

I concluded that until those in leadership roles at the various colleges and universities begin to explore academic, racial, and other inequities and take a more comprehensive and sincere approach to addressing these problems, the status quo will remain the same. In the meantime, the revenue-generating colleges and universities will continue to profit at a rate of tens or perhaps hundreds of millions of dollars annually across the broad spectrum of collegiate athletics. In the meantime, Black male student-athletes will continue to linger behind the general student population when it comes to earning their degrees. Dismal though the situation is, there are steps the leadership at various colleges and universities could and should take to reverse this trend, if the will is there all other resources are already in place.

In addition, another recent report titled: *Black Male Student-Athletes and Racial Inequities in NCAA Division I Revenue-Generating College Sports*, addresses the dismal graduation rate for Black male student-athletes at the top seven NCAA Division I universities of major collegiate sports conferences (Harper, Williams, Blackman, 2016). Among the report's recommendations is the need to demand transparency from key booster clubs for many of the major revenue-generating universities. Unbeknown to many, college and university boosters play a critical role and contribute to the demise of the Black male student-athlete once he is no longer able to perform athletically for their school. It is not my intent to paint all booster clubs or organizations with the same brush; however, the vast majority of these organizations contribute "conditionally" financially and in other ways by providing goods and services as long as these young men run, jump, shoot, for the colleges or universities they support.

With the exception of those few Black male student-athletes who have: 1. performed for top Division I and II colleges and universities and have opportunities to actually earn a tryout for a professional sports team; and/or 2. have family members, friends, or acquaintances' who are situated where they can make personnel decisions (i.e., hiring, promoting, etc.), many Black male student-athletes will find themselves among the tens or perhaps hundreds of thousands of former student-athletes who did not graduate with their college degrees and are unable to find work in their field of study and/or areas of interests. A primary reason for such dismal outcomes can be directly linked to members of this group lacking proper information. Well-known activist, author, and lecturer the late great Richard Gregory, aka Dick Gregory, reminds his worldwide audiences of the importance of having the "right information."

Unfortunately, Black male student-athletes may very well find themselves as victims of this phenomenon which I refer to as a lack of correct information with apertures or gaps. Furthermore, when athletically talented Black male student-athletes acquire the navigational skills to successfully steer clearly amid the realities of the terrain they are faced with, it is at this juncture they realize as the late great Sam Cooke sang; "A Change Is Going to Come!"

This chapter is meant to ignite your thinking about your college/university experience to date. What comes to mind when you think about your reason(s) for going to college? Were you more interested in what you could accomplish academically, athletically, or both? What or who influenced you the most when it came time for you to select a college/university? Were you more attracted to the academic or athletic program offerings at the college/university you attend/attended? Are you still a student or did you drop out before earning your degree? If you are still a student-athlete are your goals geared toward degree completion, regardless of what happens athletically? If you dropped out what were your reason(s)? Have you considered returning to complete your degree? If you answered yes to the previous question—great! If you have not considered returning to complete what you started, why not?

# Energy Investment

This chapter ends with the Black Male Student-Athlete's Self-Assessment Survey. Your responses to the survey questions will hopefully help you to at least begin thinking about alternatives to entering the professional sports arena. As the book title states, there are alternatives to the pros and one can be a "pro" in a plethora of industries outside of the professional sports arena. Think about what it takes to be a pro and consider the definition of a professional: One who has specialized training, skill, education, desire, and determination to efficiently perform a task(s) at a high level. Those qualifications are not reserved for professional athletes only. Whether you know it or not, your pursuit of your college degree can and will prepare you to become a professional in any industry you choose, especially if you do not make the pros!

It is not my intention to discourage you if you aspire to become a professional athlete. After all, "one must listen to the music within!" When one "listens to their music within" the pursuit of one's goal(s) becomes something that he wakes up every day and look forward to pursuing that "music within." The point is that when one does this, work becomes a labor of love and never feels like work! I do this every day and am doing it as I write this book. I pray that this book will help readers to consider the topics broached throughout the book.

## Where do/did you invest the most energy: in the classroom or on the field/court?

It has been said that if you watch what someone does more than anything else, you can identify where their passion lies. Every day each of us devotes a certain amount of energy; we tend to devote the most energy to what is most important to us. For example, I devote most of my daily energy to writing, speaking, and mentoring Black males in general and Black male student-athletes in particular. As a student-athlete where do you devote most of your attention and energies during a typical day? Understandably, as a student-athlete you exert a certain amount of physical and mental energy to practicing and playing your sport. However, when you take an honest assessment, how do you measure up? Would you say that you devote more energy to your academic activities than you do to your athletic activities? Are you scheduled to graduate on time based on your current routine? If you answered yes, great! However, if you are not on schedule to graduate on time, are you taking advantage of the various student support services available to you? If you are falling behind in your classes have you considered speaking with your academic advisor and/or your athletic liaison to arrange tutoring? There is no shame is asking for help, we are all ignorant of something. For example, have you reWquested an extension on the assignment(s) that you may be falling behind in? These are simply suggestions for you to think about accessing if needed.

One overlooked strategy that many students and Black male student athletes fail to capitalize on is developing relationships with their professors. In addition to teaching the course(s), most professors would be happy to sit and discuss ways and means for you to have a successful outcome in their classes, even if you have fallen behind because of your participation in athletic events. By taking this approach you send the message to your professor(s) that your academic success is just as important or more important than your success as a student-athlete.

My personal experience as an associate professor of business for the past 10 years confirms the fact that when a student communicates with me about having challenges personally and academically, I work with them to identify potential solutions to their dilemma(s), whatever they may be. However, if a student is having challenges such as falling behind in a course(s) and does not communicate and ask for guidance, he is doomed to fail.

Therefore, when you consider and begin to employ all or some of the strategies outlined in this book, your chances of becoming a successful student-athlete are increased exponentially.

I hope you are/were not affected by the "Black Dumb Jock Syndrome." "Dumb jocks" are not born, they are being systematically created. Black student-athletes suffer from the outset from disadvantages: the myth of innate Black athletic superiority, the stereotype of the dumb Black, and social forces determining a vulnerability to exploitation (Edwards, 1984). I truly hope that this phenomenon has not affected you and caused you to not take seriously the academic portion of your experience in high school or college.

## Questions to ponder:

1. When if ever did you think about the possibility of becoming a professional athlete?

2. Did you really give thought to any industry other than a professional sports franchise?

3. At what point did you decide that you wanted to attend a college or university?

4. What attracted you to the school the most?

5. Were you approached by a scout or a member of an athletic team, or did you receive offers or letters of interest while in high school?

# Black Male Student-Athletes' Self-Assessment Survey

1.  When if ever, did you think about the possibility of being a professional athlete?

**Response:**

2.  Did you really give thought to any industry other than a professional sports franchise? If yes, what industry(s)? If not, why not?

**Response:**

3.  While in high school at what point did you decide that you wanted to attend the college or university you are currently attending or attended?

**Response:**

4.  What attracted you most to your current/former school? Was it athletics or academics, or both?

**Response:**

5. Were you approached by a scout or a member of an athletic team, or did you receive offers or letters of interest while in high school?

**Response:**

6. Prior to entering your current/former college/university, did you or others consider you the best athlete in your region? If yes, why? If not, why not?

**Response:**

7. As a current/former college/university student-athlete have you prepared for and considered being a "pro" in an industry other than professional sports?

**Response:**

If career guidance from a seasoned career guidance professional could be provided, would you be willing to accept professional guidance?
Yes_____ No_____

CHAPTER TWO

# Taking an Honest Self-Assessment

This chapter is offered to ignite your thinking about your college or university experiences. For clarity when I use the term college it includes universities and other secondary institutions. What comes to your mind when you think about your reasons for going to college? Were you more interested in what you might accomplish academically? Or were you more interested in your athletic prowess? Perhaps you were equally interested in academics and athletics? What or who influenced you the most when it came time for you to select a particular college? Or did you feel a nearly equal attraction to the academic and athletic program offerings at that college?

There was a self-assessment survey at the end of chapter one, and I am reintroducing the survey at the end of this chapter as well, to help you take a good look inside of yourself. Your honesty responding to the survey will be critical to your ability to look at "your truth" as it pertains to your academic and athletic goals. Hopefully, this chapter will help you to ease any reluctance you may have felt when you first looked at the survey.

When I speak about honesty with self, I had to get myself on track years ago because I allowed the streets to dictate my every move. As you begin reading the next section of this chapter see if you can identify with portions of my journey. And, if you find yourself in need of assistance because of certain impediments you have come up against, your honesty with self will help to guide you to those who are willing and can assist you, no matter what your issue(s) may be. Remember, when you are willing to do the right thing for the right reasons the Universe will put people in your path to help you. There will be impediments in your path, I assure you; however, how you handle those impediments will be the keys to your success, only if you are willing to say, "I need help!"

## Roadblocks

In this section here are some of the impediments that I had to overcome in order to get my life on the right track. I wrote about the "full ride" scholarship offers I had as a high school junior playing varsity basketball, and how I had several scholarship offers; however, because of my physical and mental condition I could not accept them. It was at this point I realized that I needed help. Fortunately, there were people in my life who helped me and believe me, there were several things that I needed to try and overcome. Being honest with myself allowed me to take a survey as you have been asked to take, and it is one that has helped several young men like yourself.

The first thing I had to do was to get honest with myself and realize I needed help.

As a high school junior playing varsity basketball, I began receiving letters of interest from various colleges and universities throughout the country. It was at that point that I gave thought to the possibility of attending college on a basketball scholarship. I performed exceptionally well on the basketball court as a member of a team that was ranked at one point the 11th best high school basketball team in the U.S. During those days, the technology was yet to be as developed as it is now, however, despite the absence of technology the old Associated Press teletypes were the primary mode of nationwide communication. Unfortunately, my life off the court was in shambles, primarily because of my daily use of heroin which eventually led to my abysmal performance and my exit from the high school team at the urging of my high school varsity basketball coach. I wish I could share that the coach's act was one of compassion and care. But I soon discovered that his resentment toward me was intense, since I had in his mind jeopardized his chances of being acknowledged as a premier basketball coach in the region and nation. As a 6'6" guard/forward who according to many was the best outside shooter on the team, my coach realized that my contributions were needed to help ensure his success. Of those fans and supporters who are still around today, they still talk about how I was "hitting three's" (three-point shots) long before the advent of the three-point shot was conceived in the minds of the basketball "gods."

After being dismissed from my high school team in 1968, my troubles with drug use began to escalate. In early 1968 I was arrested for possession and distribution of heroin and needed help legally and treatment-wise. Fortunately, my mother served as a domestic worker for a prominent attorney whose son was a big fan of mine. When he discovered my situation, my young fan spoke with his father and asked if he could help me. Upon discovering that I was the son of his domestic worker, the attorney asked my mother if he could be of service. Knowing full well that my mother could not afford attorney's fees, the attorney decided to take my case pro bono (cost free). While being arraigned in City Court on the drug charges the attorney came forward and informed the court that he would be acting as my attorney. The attorney requested and was granted a brief recess to introduce himself, discuss my case with the judge and district attorney and to make me an offer. Since I was facing my second set of charges within the same week my chances of being released on my own recognizance (ROR'd) were nil.

Next came a most astonishing offer: the attorney said he would inform the court that he would take responsibility for my conduct and behavior. I recall thinking to myself: this guy is special. His next offer was even more astonishing, with my permission he would inform the court that I would reside with him and his family, and he would pay out of pocket to have tutors come and teach me in his home so that I could complete my high school education. It was just Mom and I because my father had died in 1967, and Mom had no place else to turn. My desire to avoid going to prison made it easy to accept his offer to live with him and his family. They lived in the wealthiest part of New Rochelle, New York, and my accommodations were excellent. I had the entire third floor to myself, complete with my own entrance.

For the next 18 months, I resided with the attorney and his family and was treated as a member of the family. Yet, as a member of the Jewish culture, my attorney understood that as a Black man with different cultural leanings I needed and wanted to interact with my own friends. I was encouraged to invite and hang out with my own friends, and I was told that they were welcome in their home at any time. At the time, I could not have admitted that my drug problem was greater than even I realized. Therefore, periodically I would venture back to my neighborhood and continued using drugs.

At the end of my 18 months' stay with the attorney and his family, we mutually agreed that it was time for me to return home to live with my mom. Although I continued to play ball in various summer leagues, I didn't complete my high school education until I was 22 years of age, when I successfully earned my General Equivalency Diploma (GED) issued by the New York State Department of Education in 1973.

## A Growing Basketball Talent

My first realization that my athletic skills were higher than most.

As my junior year in high school was ending, I began giving serious thought to playing at the next level, which in this case meant going to college. As my playing career continued, I began playing against tougher competition. Of interest to me was my ability to compete against some of the best high school and college players in the New York City area. During those days, those players included: Nate (Tiny) Archibald, Charlie Scott, Walter Davis, Willie and Mike Sojourner, and Lew Alcindor's (later known as Kareem Abdul Jabbar) replacement at New York City's Power Memorial High School, a young man named Len Elmore. All the above-mentioned men later had careers in the National Basketball Association (NBA).

It was during a preseason scrimmage in 1968 against perennial national basketball powerhouse Power Memorial High School where I began to seriously believe that my playing skills was on par with some of the best high school basketball players in the country. Len Elmore was the center and matched up against my dear late friend Bob Kershaw. Kershaw "ate Elmore's lunch" that day! Although I forget the name of the starting small forward on that team, what I do recall was he and I "checked" (guarded) each other and I too had much success in that scrimmage. Not only did we win what may have appeared to many to be a meaningless preseason scrimmage, in my mind that day I realized that I could compete with the best players in the country.

When was your first realization that your athletic skills were higher than most?

When you assess your own athletic skills, how do you measure up? Do you consider yourself to be the best athlete in your city, state, region? Where do you rank nationally? Do you seek out the best competition to compete against, and how do/did you fare against greater competition?

# Regrets

I asked a friend of mine those questions. He played seven years in the NBA and parts of his story appears in this book. When he and I spoke about his being recruited, he stated that as a high school junior he was contacted by several representatives from various colleges and universities. My friend, whom I will call the "chairman of the boards" was 6'9" and 210 pounds, eventually decided to attend the University of Minnesota.

During our many talks over the years about life in general and regrets since we are both senior citizens now, he speaks often about how he regrets not earning his degree while attending the University of Minnesota with a full scholarship! In addition, after "retiring" from the NBA after playing only seven years, my friend recalled the countless times he applied for positions and was denied opportunities because he did not complete his college education which by the way did not cost him a dime because of the full scholarship he was awarded. As a result, he has not been able to maintain meaningful employment over the years. It is extremely important as a student-athlete that degree completion is paramount to your ability to become a professional in any number of industries.

Therefore, if after conducting an honest assessment of your athletic abilities and "honestly" determining whether you have a chance to become a professional athlete, all is not lost. As stated throughout this book, there are alternatives to becoming a "pro" outside of the professional sports arena. Completing your academic studies helps to ensure that you can have a successful and meaningful post-college career. Moreover, your ability to use the skills you have developed over the years as a student-athlete can provide you with a prominent place in industries such as those involved with science, technology, engineering, and mathematics (STEM). If you have an interest in one or more of these subjects, be sure that you focus your course of study in at least one of these areas to help ensure your success as a professional when you enter the job market. Another option that is available to you, would be to work for yourself as an entrepreneur, more on this topic in chapter nine.

Below you will find the Black Male Student-Athletes' Self-Assessment Survey. When you revisit the survey, your responses will hopefully help you to you take an honest look at where you are currently and more importantly, where you want to go when you complete your college career. Whatever decision(s) you make, know that you are not alone.

# Black Male Student-Athletes' Self-Assessment Survey
# Part II

1. Have you ever made excuses for not playing when you knew that your opponent(s) were better than you?

**Response:**

2. Is it your goal or your dream to one day play professional sports?

**Response:**

3. Regardless of the particular sport(s) you play, have you ever felt intimidated by a teammate or opponent?

**Response:**

4. If you were intimated, why were you intimated and where did you "sense" the intimation the most, was it in your head or your heart?

**Response:**

5.  Have you ever tried or were you successful in intimating an oppo-
    nent or teammate?

**Response:**

6.  What does intimidation feel like when you are the target of such an
    act?

**Response:**

7.  Can you recall the times that you felt intimidated, was it your oppo-
    nent or teammate(s) who tried or succeeded in their quest to intim-
    idate you? How did it feel?

**Response:**

If career guidance from a seasoned career guidance professional could be
provided, would you be willing to accept professional guidance?
Yes____ No__

Note: The author understands that intimidation is a "tool" in the toolbox
of an athlete, it is important for the student athlete to consider, what
happens if his attempt(s) at intimating fails.

CHAPTER THREE

# Peer Comparison Academically and Athletically

As a student-athlete how often do you compare yourself with your peers academically and athletically? When you play/played street ball as well as in various school settings, both high school and college, how do/did you measure up? Comparing yourself to those whom you compete with and against is only natural for athletes. However, there is another component that should be questioned and at times challenged. For example, how often do you compare your academic status with those whom you compete against athletically? For those of you who are headed to a college or university, were you approached by a coach or scout? If you were, what part of your interaction with the school representative focused on your academic status? When discussing your academic status were you comfortable with the discussions? Did you feel that the athletic representative offered to provide a holistic approach to your athleticism and academic responsibilities as it pertained to his or her offer? Or did you feel that you were not required to focus as much on your academic responsibilities as on your participation in sports? Other than competing against your peers in the athletic arena, whether it's football or basketball, the two major sports that Black male student-athletes participate in, how often do/did you discuss your primary reason for planning to or attending a college or university? There is a reason that the term "student-athlete" is used. As a student-athlete how are you measuring up as a student compared to your athletic participation?

## Assessment and Reality Check

At this point, it is incumbent upon me to discuss the systemic miseducation of Black males through schooling and sports, which begins much earlier than when they walk onto a college or university campus for the first time. When it comes to the academic side of the student-athlete's holistic development many tend to blame the student-athlete for their academic under-preparedness and failures. Granted, the student-athlete themselves have a responsibility to prepare themselves academically for the road ahead as it pertains to addressing their academic shortcomings. Harrison, Bimper, Smith, & Logan (2017) argue that what occurred at the middle school levels illuminates mismatched identities and the miseducation many young Black males received as far back as when they were in middle school and high school, thus laying the groundwork for academic failure at the college level. Unless and until administrators, those in athletic leadership positions as well as instructors are willing to modify the ways in which they instruct Black males, this continuum of failure will continue.

One of the first steps that needs to be taken was thoroughly laid out by Kunjufu (2011), in his excellent work, *Understanding Black Male Learning Styles*. Also, according to a 2010 report from the Schott Foundation for Public Education, when it comes to peer comparison academically among Black male students, researchers and scholars highlight the fact that one out of every two Black males will not matriculate past the secondary level. The report also pinpoints broader societal issues based primarily on the continuing neglect and stigmatizing of Black males' academic prowess and their ability to develop holistically (Howard, 2014; Noguera, 2008). During the 2007–2008 school year, Black males' in general graduation rates was 31 percent lower than White males who graduated at a rate of 78 percent, an astounding difference of 47 percent for Black males (Schott Foundation for Public Education, 2010). Sadly, Black male student athlete's graduation rates tend to be even lower than that of Black male student who do not serve as athletes.

For those student-athletes who may have their eyes open on going to the pros, it's important to first search within yourself, and we have already discussed the importance of taking this step by doing the self-assessment survey. I will remind you again of the factual reasons why earning your degree should be paramount in your mind. For example, "the chances of becoming a professional athlete for Black males is 2 out of 100,000 or .00002 percent" (Cooper, 2019, p. 62). Another way to look at this is there are roughly 21.5 million Black men in the U.S. according to Cooper (2019) and 2017 U.S. Census data. Of the 21.5 million Black men in the U.S., there are less than 1,500 on NBA and NFL rosters. Despite this reality, you must be aware that mass media coverage suggests that a majority of adult Black males in the U.S. are professional athletes. This is both a fallacious and egregious assertion.

Generally speaking, from an athletic perspective, Black male student-athletes generally compare themselves when competing in street ball settings, which is usually accompanied by playground "trash talking." Moreover, the extent of veracity of the academic discussions, if at all, are generally centered around what college or university one aspires to attend. Such decisions are more often than not focused the reputation the college or university has, especially when it comes to basketball and football primarily. However, for those Black male student-athletes who have received one or more letters of interest from colleges or universities, this immediately raises the bar as it pertains to the intensity of the trash talking in the street ball arena. It is during these types of discussion where one's competitive juices begin to flow and the verbal and both formal and informal "debates" take place. At some point during these debates/ trash talking sessions, classroom academic performances are discussed at a minimal, if at all.

One day while observing a pickup game that ended shortly thereafter, I saw my opportunity to inject into the conversations of whose game was better, and I made an inquiry to no one in particular. I had overheard one of the brother's saying that he would like to attend an Ivy League school. Of course, I immediately thought of Columbia University, an Ivy League university in the heart of Harlem, New York. I asked the brothers who were resting before starting their next run and who were mostly high school students, have you taken or are you scheduled to take your American College Test more commonly known as the ACT examination, or the Scholastic Aptitude Test commonly known as the S.A.T. examination both are standardized test that determines a high school graduate's academic preparedness for college?

After a seemingly long pause, a hush went out over the players assembled. One young brother asked, "What's the ACT OR THE sat got to do with going to college?"

I thought, what an excellent "teaching moment" for me. Of particular interest to me was the brother who had expressed an interest in attending Columbia University, an Ivy League school right there in his neighborhood. Once it was clear that those gathered were "tuned in," I asked the brother, "Has your guidance counselor spoken to you about the ACT or SAT exams?

He said none of his counselors or coaches had mentioned anything to him about the importance of studying and preparing to take one or both of those exams. At that point I suggested that he speak with his guidance counselor about taking one or both those exams. As our discussion come to a close, I asked the brothers to contact me to let me know the results of their conversations with their guidance counselors.

# Filling in the Gap

Now that you have this information, what should be your next steps? I will share my thoughts based on my experience over the years working with Black males both student athletes and non-athletes as well. Although this is not detailed in the self-assessment survey, here is a formula that I suggest you try, by doing some self-introspection on yourself. If you are currently playing for a college or university, how well are you doing academically and athletically? Are you the best player on your team, in your conference? Have you been recognized on the national stage? How often do you or have you sought out competition that you know is better than you at this point in your academic athletic journey? Have you had a heart-to heart with your coaches, if yes, what are they saying about your chances of going pro?

Here is the big question: Is your participation in athletics having a negative impact on your academic performance? It is vitally important that you do not allow the current opportunity you have as a student-athlete to slip through your fingers. The one thing that you will be able to count on is having your degree in hand when you graduate from your college or university!

Think about all the student-athletes you have known who thought they would make the pros and did not even get a call from a pro team, yet they left school early without their degree in hand. Of those student-athletes you know or have known, although I do not know any of you personally, I can state that I know those who left school early to try for the pros did not make it! And how many of those brothers returned to complete their studies and earn their degree? Those who left before earning their degrees often find themselves in dead-end jobs or doing menial work for less pay than they need or deserve.

During my 30+ years working with Black male student-athletes and living in New York City, I see many of them on several occasions as I travel from one borough to another. At times I come to tears silently when I see some of these brothers. Most of them had "full ride" scholarships because of their athletic talent and focused very little if any attention on their academic progress leading to graduation. When I see these brothers standing on the street corners, aka the block, many of them are either drinking alcohol daily or coming in and out of the various drug dens that can be found all over New York City. When I do catch them sober, I will hang out on the block with them and we talk. Interestingly, every brother with whom I speak who was once football or basketball star at their school and did not make the pros, they often say to me, "Charlie (or as I am known by most as Dr. C.), I feel so bad that I dropped out without earning my degree." They believe that their mental, psychological, and spiritual pain is so much, they drink alcohol daily and do drugs daily to "dull the pain" of their failure.

Today's academic institutions have so many ways and methods for adults to return and complete their degrees and all it takes on their part is to make the effort to return. I speak from experience. I returned 25 years later to complete my baccalaureate degree after starting and leaving school 25 years earlier. Therefore, I remind the brothers on street corners that they too can return and complete their degree work. Life can and will get better when you have that degree aka sheepskin in hand. I listen to them tell me what can only be described as horror stories. After a while I move on because I identify with what they are going through and oftentimes feel somewhat helpless to help them because the best I can do in the moment is offer then a few dollars, which usually end up in the hands of a liquor or drug merchant. However, before I go, I leave them my business card and encourage them to call me. I tell them I am positioned to help them, only if they are willing to make a sincere effort to turn their lives around. On what can only be described as very rare occasions do I hear from these brothers and it is usually a call to "borrow" money. My usual reply to such request is, I do not loan money to anyone, that is why when I see them, I give money with no expectation of the money being returned.

I share this with my readers in the hope that some brothers may realize that all is not lost. You can fill the gap between your dream of becoming a sports pro and the reality of where you stand athletically and academically. After all, W.I.N. is an acronym for What's Important Now! This is why I emphasize the value of completing that college degree work. Earning a college degree can be challenging, especially to those student-athletes who did not receive a proper foundational high school education that prepared them for college. Later in the book we discuss the value of grade point averages (GPA).

## Academic Comparisons with Peers

How often do you discuss you GPA with your fellow Black male students-athletes? Or is the focus on athletic talent and skills only? It is understandable that some of you may be ashamed or not proud of your grade point average. If you are a student-athlete who is only interested in making sure that he does not lose his eligibility, perhaps you should rethink that position. What happens if you get injured, which we all know can occur at any time. If you find yourself in such a situation, you usually have created more pressure on yourself academically. Not being able to participate athletically should not prevent you from having a successful experience academically. Although you probably would have doctors' appointments to deal with your injury and depending on your level of pain or discomfort, it may be difficult to focus on your studies in a way that is required to earn good grades. There is a plethora of opportunities for you to get assistance if needed. Moreover, there are many on-campus support services and various clubs and organizations with which you should familiarize yourself with. Many of these clubs and organizations are there to provide support to all students. Perhaps while you are recovering from an injury you can contact the office of student support services on your campus and receive one-on-one academic assistance with assignments, preparing papers and other academic related activities.

The point is, no matter how well you perform as an athlete, unless you have put the same effort and energy into your academic studies, only then can you assure yourself of having better outcomes as opposed to an unwillingness to focus on and complete your academic studies. If you ask, I can guarantee you there is always someone to help you academically, just as there are to help you athletically.

Peer comparison academically and athletically can often take one to places that may be internally uncomfortable. For this reason, honestly assessing one's self is so critical to the holistic growth and development of the Black male student-athlete (Cooper, 2019). Think about this; of all the student-athletes you have known, how many of them did you think you were better than athletically and yet they failed to make it to the pros? How will your life be altered if you do not get a call/visit from a representative of a professional sports organization? Are you a student who happens to be an athlete, or are you an athlete who happens to be a student? Perhaps to date you have not given serious thought to these questions; however, I strongly encourage you to do so. Of course, by now if you have reached your sophomore or junior year in college, do you already have an idea of your talent level when it comes to your pro prospects in sports? Of the many young men whom I have known and worked with over the past three decades, one of the things I realized after speaking to and spending time with them was that many admitted they never considered many of the topics posed in this book, especially when it comes to alternatives to the professional sports arenas.

Failure to consider many of the questions and topics posed here could have lifelong negative ramifications in your life. I make this statement with the utmost humility and in a totally nonjudgmental manner. Sharing some of my personal and tragic experiences as a young ball player, is done to hopefully help you to realize the value of an *honest* self-assessment, and it should not be minimized. Proper guidance by a competent career professional is vital to you not only as a student-athlete, but also as a young man entering the most important developmental phase of your life, young adulthood.

Although the self-assessment in chapter two covered this already, for the sake of clarity and thoroughness I believe the topic of what attracted you the most to your current college/university is worth revisiting. When thinking about your pre-college days, what comes to mind when you think about how and why you ended up at the college/university you attend/attended? Did you spend time researching both the academic and athletic potential your school offered you as a student-athlete? Many of the successful former student-athletes to whom I have spoken over the years often tell me they realized after their freshman and sophomore years in college that they needed to "buckle down" on their academic responsibilities. Although one can be sincerely dedicated to both their academic and athletic performance, by the time one reaches their sophomore year in college there should be or should have been indicators of what the best area of focus should be or should have been as it pertained to selecting a major or area of interest.

Comparing yourself with your peers, athletically and academically, is understandable and a natural part of young adulthood, especially if you are an athlete. However, as we will explore further in upcoming chapters, by delving deeply into your interests outside of playing pro sports will hopefully lead you to take an honest self-assessment that can help target your skill set into a profession in any industry.

To help my student-athlete readers develop a better sense of where they rate academically and athletically, I urge you to focus on and seriously consider the questions posed at the end of the chapter. The primary purpose of these questions is to give student-athletes an opportunity to conduct an honest self-assessment of where they rate when compared to their peers academically and athletically.

**Questions to ponder:**

1.  What is similar and different in the academic and athletic comparisons you make among your peers?

**Response:**

2.  How do you rate in both areas?

**Response:**

3.  What feelings emerge when you reflect on those comparisons?

**Response:**

4.  When you compare and contrast your feelings, how do they contribute to your view of your fellow Black male student-athletes? How do feel when you're on campus? Are you comfortable being there? Do you feel like you belong there or not? Are you concerned with how you are viewed or not?

**Response:**

5.  What comes to mind when you do some self-exploration on how you are viewed. What are the results?

**Response:**

6. Many Black male student-athletes feel like they are just "studs" on their campus and are viewed as such by other students and even the administration. If you have these feelings, what do you do with them?

**Response:**

7. At this point in your academic and athletic career, where have you or did you perform best, academically or athletically?

**Response:**

8. What feelings do you experience while conducting this "honest" assessment of where you stand?

**Response:**

9. Where does your assessment place you as a student and as an athlete?

**Response:**

How do you self-identify, as a student first, or as an athlete who happens to be a student?

**Response:**

The questions you been encouraged to ponder above are there to help you to pay attention to your feelings. And, to remind you that your primary goal should be to earn your degree come hell or high water! Your answers to these questions may guide you in your next steps.

# CHAPTER FOUR

# Industry of Interest Outside of Playing Professional Sports

I n this section we will explore alternatives to becoming a player for a professional sports organization. If your passion for sports is such that you would consider taking an alternative role to playing professional sports while remaining in the professional sports arena, your formal education could be a huge factor in entering the professional sports arena in another capacity. For example, if your area of interest/major in college was/is in the counseling field, finance, scouting, and personnel to name a few positions available in all professional sports organizations, having your degree enhances your chance of serving in the capacity of a paid professional exponentially. If, however, your interest lies elsewhere, for instance, if you have a propensity for working with figures, all sports organizations have a need for accountants, general managers, assistant general managers, public relations specialists, etc., who are skilled at tabulating, analyzing, and communicating about sports related matters data collection for example. The point is, there are a plethora of ways to enter the professional sports arena without being a player necessarily.

Earning your degree or returning to complete your degree is a definite must in order to help ensure that you can position yourself to have a successful economic outcome for you and your family. Moreover, as a current/former student-athlete your understanding of teamwork and having a "feel" for what the athletes themselves are going or have gone through can be a tremendous advantage in most industries where teamwork is a critical component for workplace success. In addition, the academic and athletic skills developed during your college career could also serve you well if you decide to become an entrepreneur by going into business for yourself. More on this later.

# The Challenges of Tunnel Vision

Although there is a plethora of reasons why challenges in general exist. However, for each challenge that exist there are generally equal opportunities for Black male student-athletes to eliminate the "tunnel vision" that many have developed during their athletic careers. One such challenge involves the strenuous schedules many have to contend with. For example, from an athletic standpoint there is the typical and oftentimes grueling training and game schedule that athletes must maintain. These athletes also have the responsibility of keeping up with their academic responsibilities. In addition to "finding time" to attend class, complete assignments and study for class discussion and exams, it's also a good idea for them to participate in campus activities such as fraternities, student academic associations and organizations to name a few. And, for those who are interested in fraternal life and study groups, an often-overlooked resource that is important for establishing relationships is found in interacting with their professors and campus staff persons.

Along with the question of how to meet those challenges is the question for many student-athletes: Is their focus on remaining academically eligible so they can continue to participate in their chosen sport, or is their focus on earning their degrees while remaining eligible to participate in the respective sport(s)? Rhoden (2006) introduced the "conveyor belt concept" as a tool used by colleges and universities to mask their exploitation of many Black male student-athletes and promote the idea of a simple, color-blind meritocracy in and through sport. I support the need to broadening Black male student-athletes' vision and help reduce the tunnel vision that too many of them have regarding their participation in the professional sports arena. In addition, Rhoden (2006) provides examples of the realities of Black male student-athletes' chances of turning pro before or after completing their academic studies.

## Chances as a Sports Pro

The chances for Black male student-athletes to become professional athletes are dismal. According to Leonard and Reyman (1988), two out of every 100,000 or .00002 percent of Black male student-athletes have an opportunity to become professional athletes. In accordance with the most recently available data from the U.S. Census Bureau (2017), there are 21.5 million Black men in the U.S. and there are less than 1,500 Black males on the National Basketball Association and National Football League rosters on any given year.

This means that the percentage of Black males in the NBA and NFL, out of all Black males in the U.S. population is .000000005 (U.S. Census Bureau, 2017). In spite of these statistical realities, media coverages from various platforms send a message that the majority of adult Black males in U.S. society are professional athletes. Not only are these fallacious assertions misleading, but they also speak to and influence many Black male student-athletes by sending a message that their chances of becoming a professional athlete are exponentially higher than they really are.

## Course Offerings and Options

The following question must be explored in depth: Why is it that most colleges and universities do not feature or require courses focused on other opportunities within professional sports? Perhaps if more colleges and universities were to broaden their academic offerings to include sports law, sports medicine, sports and media, sports and history, professional sports administration and management, and other subjects, student-athletes could make more informed academic decisions. In fairness, more recently many colleges and universities have been offering more courses and even degrees in the above-mentioned prospective areas of interests. However, of the Black male student-athletes interviewed for this book the vast majority stated that they were never introduced in a serious manner to other careers available in the sports world other than participating as a professional athlete.

Let's consider one such person. Earl B. was fortunate enough to have a tryout by a professional sport franchise but failed to make "the final cut" and was released. While sitting in a local park in New York City I noticed during our discussion that tears began to well up in Earl's eyes. I paused to give Earl time to gather himself before continuing our conversation. When I asked Earl about the tears, he stated that while in college his coaches and academic counselors never broached the topic of alternatives available to him. As I probed further, Earl was in his mid-40s during the time of the discussion has a family and is eking out a living in a dead-end job stated: "My love for sports in general and basketball in particular was such that I would have welcomed the opportunity to pursue courses or a degree path that could have led me to a career path such as teaching sports to youth, community development, nonprofit development, and possibly sports financing." Sadly, Earl dropped out of college after failing to make good on the professional sports opportunity he had been given years ago (Earl S. personal communication, August 18, 2017).

Earl's story is one of many such stories told to this writer by Black male student-athletes who were misinformed or uninformed about academic opportunities that could have kept them in the industry they have loved since childhood. As I have done here and with other former Black male student athletes, I reminded Earl that it was not too late to position himself to where he could return to college and complete his degree in an area such as sports management with an emphasis on business administration and management. After all, his life experiences could play a critical role in his ability to not only pursue his long-held passion for serving in the sports industry. His story could also be critical in helping other Black male student-athletes to either stay in school or return to complete their degree work, perhaps enabling them to serve in a non-athletic role in the sports industry.

## Strategies

For those current and former Black male student athletes who may be interested in pursuing one of the many roles available and to increase their chances of landing a role in the sports industry such as those listed previously, completing your degree could help to ensure a successful career in the sports industry. In addition, during your years of participation in athletic events as a current or former student-athlete, you likely have established good relationships with athletic administrators, coaches, professors, etc. You should take advantage of the plethora of networking opportunities that you have hopefully established over the months and years. If as a student-athlete you have reached a point in your life where the real possibility of being contacted by a professional sports organization is dim, perhaps a review of your responses to the Black Male Student-Athletes' Self-Assessment Survey (BMSASAS) presented in a previous chapter could serve as a tool to help you determine if you have a realistic shot at turning pro or not.

Upon completion of your *honest* self-assessment along with the assessment in chapter five The Community of Self, it is hoped that these evaluation tools can help to guide your decision making as it pertains to taking your "next steps" in your life. In addition, I cannot stress strongly enough the value that could be found in using the relationships you have established with academic advisors or professors with whom you have developed a degree of trust, such professionals could be helpful in selecting or changing your major or area(s) of interest that best fit your desire to serve in the sports industry. This, too, can be part of your strategizing while in college.

# The Dilemma of Priorities

Many of the current and former Black male student-athletes with whom I have interacted with over the years have made such statements as, "I was told to take a major like psychology by my academic advisor because courses like psychology and sociology are 'easy' to pass. Such counsel has often led to the belief that remaining academically eligible to participate in sports was more important to the student-athlete, academic advisor, and perhaps the university's leadership who were more concerned with a student-athlete's eligibility to play than in this case his desire to pursue a degree or area of interest to which he was drawn and had a real interest in.

Further probing led me to some interesting responses from student-athletes who were "steered" in a direction that best fit their ability to remain academically eligible to play sports, just in case the National Collegiate Athletic Association (N.C.A.A.) decided to pop in to review academic records. For example, several student-athletes expressed their desires to major in disciplines within the sports arena, such as those mentioned previously, such sports law, sports business administration, management, sports medicine, sports finance, sports nonprofit leadership development, to name a few. However, the response from many of these student-athletes went something like this: I really wanted to major in sports management, sports finance, or sports technology just in case I did not receive an offer from a professional sports organization. Once again, they were faced with what Joseph N. Cooper, PhD discussed in-depth in his excellent book, *From Exploitation Back to Empowerment: Black Male Holistic (Under) Development Through Sports and (Mis) Education* (2019). To counter the tendency toward having tunnel vision and to maximize the ability to undergo a transformative rather than an exploitative, experience while in college, there seems to be a need for guidance counselors who operate independently from sports departments, who understand the dilemma Black male student-athletes go through as they try to prioritize between being students and being athletes. These guidance counselors should support Black male student-athletes' ability to self-assess and strategize on behalf of their future.

# Matching Your Personality Type and College Major with Career Choices

How will your major academic interest match up with what you would really like to do, if becoming a professional athlete is not in the foreseeable future? For example, what areas or industries do you have a passion for serving in outside of becoming a professional athlete? Perhaps you could consider a career in science, technology, engineering, or mathematics (also known as S.T.E.M. based curriculums and degrees), along with the additional subjects introduced earlier in the chapter. Such industries offer an excellent career path that could afford opportunities for you to earn a good living for yourself and your family. Furthermore, once you identify an area or industry that you are passionate about serving in, you will never have to "work" another day in your life. I can personally bear witness to this fact in my life! Every day the Creator awakens me; for the past 30 plus years I have had the opportunity to do what I am currently doing, helping Black male student-athletes and that is called a "labor of love!"

In the next chapter readers will be asked to further their introspection into themselves with The Community of Self and will be discussed in detail. In my opinion this may be the most important chapter in the book. As a reader you will decide the value of understanding your "community of self."

**Questions to ponder:**

1.  During your course of study, what courses did you perform best in?

**Response:**

2.  If you were involved in on-campus activities, which activities or organizations were you affiliated and why?

**Response:**

3. If you were not involved in on-campus activities, why not?

**Response:**

4. Did your academic and athletic responsibilities prevent you from participating in the many campus activities, events, or organizations?

**Response:**

5. How many of your acquaintances/friends were not involved or interested in athletic activities or events, or sports in general?

**Response:**

# The Community of Self

U nbeknown to many, our spiritual lives play an important role in the totality of all of our accomplishments. Because no two people are alike, each of us has a range of components operating within us. This range of components generally operates on two different levels within every human being. For example, each of us has both conscious and sub-conscious ranges of thoughts, feelings, and emotions, primarily, inner components that make up our "community of self." Throughout each day of our lifetime, we are always operating in one of the two spheres, conscious and subconscious. Moreover, we can easily identify the conscious sphere, however, some would argue that the sub-conscious is oftentimes more powerful than our conscious selves.

To better understand our spheres, which are three-dimensional, we need look no further than our bodies. For example, each body is composed of length, width, and height and therefore is a three-dimensional sphere, and serves as an equidistant, centermost space that each person has. As an example, we are all considered to be equidistant meaning equal distance from the sun, no matter where we are located on the planet. Throughout our daily lives our actions, the feelings we encounter, respond to, and think about help to describe our community of self. Many refer to this method as "soul searching." Most of the time we use these components without using much conscious energy; however, a certain amount of energy is used regardless, although it may not appear to be. It does not matter if we are using energy consciously or subconsciously. Along with an individual's use of these various components, there is an interconnectedness, which is a state of being connected to each other and should be acknowledged.

## The Motors of Self

Drives and instincts are the earliest "citizens" of the self-community. These drives can be categorized under two major types. The first drive we will consider is the drive toward what gives satisfaction and pleasure. The other drive is just the opposite of the first and moves one away from pain and/or dissatisfaction. These drives are akin to and could be compared to our "mental speakers" for the physical body and its needs. Although, for example, our need for physical food is necessary for our survival, there is also a need for a mental representation.

Here is an example of how the mental representation works to help meet our physical needs. Before taking any physical action, the brain first sends a signal to the body that one may be hungry for physical food. Anything that could damage the physical borders of the "self" is usually experienced as painful. For example, if we are involved in an automobile collision, have cuts or burns, the entire community (the self) becomes motivated immediately and has one of two reactions to take flight or fight. Such reactions can be triggered by previous dangers or dangerous situations which immediately call in the entire physical and mental self. Alerted by memory, reason, senses, and ego, the reactions focus their specialized capacity on the threat itself.

On the other hand, there is the drive to seek pleasure and satisfaction. We learn to seek things that may have brought pleasure previously. For example, money is not in and of itself pleasurable; however, because money provides many physical pleasures, most people are driven to acquire more money. We must remain cognizant of the drives that rule the self. For instance, if the drives are allowed free rein and are only concerned with physical pleasures like food, sex, and physical relaxation, the entire community of self becomes conditioned to only seek pleasurable activities. Conversely, having an awareness of one's fear can come to rule the self and a constant state of nervousness or anxiousness could set in, causing a persistent drive to avoid pain which could create an imbalance in the self. Perhaps that old adage often associated with pain, "there is no gain without pain" has to be tempered with discretion. Therefore, rulership of one's community of self can be very limiting if a person is bound only by physical pleasures or pains.

The question must be asked about the role of the mind: If one is ruled solely by physical existence, does this limit the mind's contributions to the community of self? The opportunity for further growth and development could gain some satisfaction using the sensory connectedness between one's inner needs and outer objects. There is no doubt that the senses are a critical part of the community of self. However, if the community of self relies solely on the senses to serve as the ruler of self, the self-suffers. Akbar (1985) argues that the senses alone provide incomplete information about things which conceivably endanger the entire community of self. Therefore, one must conclude that although the senses are an important part of the community, the senses alone could make a poor ruler of self.

# Identifying a Sense of Relevance for Black Male Student-Athletes

At this juncture the Black male student-athlete may be wondering how the "community of self" fits with his dreams, aspirations, and goals. Try thinking about this from the perspective of a basketball player who is a great shooter but lacks overall scoring ability. Using the same scenario, think of the teammate who can only play well on the defensive end of the court, but lacks the ability to score consistently. In this instance, the development and growth of the community of self helps to enable both players to focus not only on what these two players do well, but also helps us to perceive what it may take for those who are willing to work on areas that offer the ability to become a better all-around player. Using all the principles outlined in this chapter can surely contribute to a student-athletes intra-connectedness within oneself as well as their interconnectedness.

## The Emotional Ego

Understanding the role of the emotional ego should be of concern to Black male student-athletes who are at a critical point in their lives and careers. The ego is another prominent member of the community of self. The ego has a specialized function, which is to make sure there is no violation of individual needs while remaining astutely aware of the potential dangers to the self. In addition, the ego can rule in a tyrannical fashion over the entire community of self.

The primary tool used by the ego is emotion. Usually when strong feelings tend to surface within the community (the self), the voice of the ego is the dominant characteristic. Furthermore, when the ego feels love, everything appears to be more beautiful and attractive. On the other hand, the ego can feel just the opposite when sadness dominates thoughts and feelings. Another of pitfalls that one can experience when the ego is gripped by negative emotions, is reasoning which usually fails to function adequately. In addition, when the ego becomes the lead emotion in someone's life they act exclusively and focus on self only. For example, what the athletes who participate in team sports tend to do often is, they take full responsibility for the outcome of an athletic event such as basketball and football.

Emotion is a type of character defect that surfaces because it is the ego's only weapon. Akbar (1985) contends that "the ego is an actor" (p. 5), most of the ego's experiences are primarily conscious acts and the ego fails to engage itself in things which it cannot see. Moreover, the ego tends to change its faces and allegiances as selfish needs may dictate. Furthermore, the ego is always committed to the best outcomes for the person and is a terrible ally for other communities of self. Although the ego is a "citizen" of the self-community, it is clearly not an appropriate ruler of the self.

## Memory

Memory is another critical component of the community of self. When memory loses sight of its position as a resource, it can try to dominate the community of self. Furthermore, memory can lose sight of its proper position and try to exert influence over the future. When this occurs, memory can become imprisoned by old memories and past experiences. Imprisonment of this nature can destroy life, primarily because the self continues to look at the present as if it were the past. When this phenomenon occurs, the past can become the ruler and old patterns of living can occur over and over (Akbar, 2015). Therefore, constantly striving to identify the proper ruler of one's community of self is a must to avoid repeating the same old patterns of thinking and acting when the outcomes can have a negative impact on one's community of self.

In addition, memory is a vital part of the community of self. Further, without memory the continuity of community can be greatly impaired. We must also be able to ascertain that when memory rules the community of self, the community tends to live in the past. Memory is akin to a library or the archives of a great city because it stores and records the experiences which are like storage bins in the basement of a large building. Think about memory in this manner, as a student-athlete who may have used a play in a game that was successful two seasons ago. When the memory is properly nourished and that "memory bank" has been maintained properly, it can always be recalled and that play can be used successfully against another opponent, or perhaps the same opponent.

# Reason

Another important member of selfhood or the community of self is reason. One's reasoning ability functions along with other members of the community of self, such as the drives, senses, ego, and memory discussed previously. For example, proper use of one's reasoning skills enables one to know that everything red is not a traffic light. Moreover, reason helps the community of self to be able to distinguish between yesterday's experiences and today's reality.

This is especially true for those Black male student-athletes who have now undertaken a true and honest self-assessment when it comes to determining their ability to function at the professional level as a paid athlete (see chapter four). This is not to suggest that you should not pursue your dream(s), however, you must use your ability to reason because reasoning can be cold and unfeeling, and judges the world based on categories and characteristics only.

Therefore, reason is an important member of the community of self. After all, there can be no self without some order and reasoning to help identify and restore one's ability to think and analyze properly. As a college or university student-athlete, developing one's reasoning skills has a place in both the classroom and on the field or court. It does not matter whether you participate in a team or individual sport, reasoning should be a highly sought out, foundational principle for developing your community of self.

Moreover, reasoning is required to make a lot of decisions. For example, if you have to choose between eating cake or eating fruit, you might use reason to determine that the cake is not good for the diet you're on, so you should choose the fruit instead. Reasoning requires the use of critical thinking skills, thought pattern alterations, recognizing and distinguishing between rational and irrational thought patterns, all of which are associated with developing one's reasoning abilities and skills.

# The Self-Accusing Spirit/Consciousness

As the self-accusing spirit or consciousness develops, a sense of justice comes to the surface. For example, the conscience polices all components of the self by introducing values of good or bad. Rather than a gentle urging for improvement, an unchecked conscience can lead to demanding nothing short of perfection, which leads to a constant state of dissatisfaction with oneself. This behavior can lead you to condemning every thought and weakness, all rising from the lower self. Your moral sense or compass, while significant, is not a be-all-and-end-all, however. Your self-accusing spirit/conscience should be a guide to your higher sense of the self-community Akbar (1985).

When one's conscience goes unchecked it can be as disruptive to the self-community as other parts discussed previously. For instance, the ego concerns itself only with the needs of the "I;" such actions impede one's ability to focus on the "We." Even the organizational sense called reason usually dominates the community of self with its rigid consistency and bows under the tempering influence of one's conscience, the sense of right and wrong.

We must be careful to improve gradually when responding to the gentle urging of the self-accusing spirit or conscience. Otherwise, as stated previously, an overdeveloped conscience can demand nothing short of perfection which can lead to a constant state of self-sacrifice. Such activity can cause one to become greedy for punishment. Therefore, one's self-accusing spirit or conscience can lead to a constant state of dissatisfaction, causing one to constantly condemn every thought, every weakness, and other drives arising from one's lower self.

The self-accusing spirit or conscience is activated by an internal clock that seems to work as a messenger, and one's response to such messages or unction's can contribute to or take away from the broader community for which we are all a part. Furthermore, the self-accusing spirit or conscience is not an end to itself but could guide one to a higher sense of self.

## Final Thoughts on the Community of Self

Unlike other creatures on earth, humans operate under a unique feature that other creatures do not possess, called the will. Unlike other creatures, the human will can free us from the limitations of our drives. Therefore, the will serves as a sort of divine representative within each person. Moreover, our willpower has the unique, remarkable function of being able to pull the mind and the flesh in the direction of your Truth!

These elements of self-community deserve our full attention. They can contribute to how we perceive ourselves, how we experience intra- and interconnectedness, how we function in everyday as well as extraordinary circumstances, and what value we place on ourselves and others. Knowing about the community of self can help you deepen your self-assessment as you move toward decisions about becoming a professional athlete, or a professional in a plethora of industries available to the one who is well prepared, of course, we are guided back to the value of completing one's formal education at the college or university level.

**Questions to ponder:**

How can your reasoning skills enhance your ability to make decisions regarding your response to the self-assessment survey presented previously in this book?

**Response:**

6. Do you understand why your ability to reason should have nothing to do with how you are feeling, but should be based on your ability to analyze a situation?

**Response:**

7. How do you respond to your self-accusing spirit or conscience when things are going well?

**Response:**

8. How often do you ignore your self-accusing spirit or conscience when in turmoil about a decision?

**Response:**

9. What do you think happens when you completely ignore the urgings of your self-accusing spirit or conscience in order to satisfy the demands of your ego? If this has happened to you, how do you feel when you recall these acts?

**Response:**

# CHAPTER SIX

# Grade Point Averages Matter

## South Carolina High School Student-Athletes and the Acceptable Grade Point Average (GPA)

I recently discovered a shocking statistic: student-athletes in my new home state of South Carolina are required to "only" maintain a grade point average of D- in order to participate in school sponsored athletic events. This kind of requirement makes a mockery of high school education in South Carolina and elsewhere throughout the country where schools accept such low academic standards from their male student athletes. Moreover, so far those in educational leadership positions refuse to address these atrocities. Of course, this is not a new phenomenon. It's simply more of the same when it comes to male student-athletes in general and Black male student-athletes in particular being used to enhance the financial coffers even at the high school level.

Such low academic standards are partly to blame for Black male student-athlete's dismal academic showings when/if they reach a college/ university campus. Coupled with an unrealistic expectation of ever reaching the professional ranks, the likelihood of most of the members of this group earning their baccalaureate degrees is dismal at best.

A weekly talk radio show in South Carolina recently invited members of the local school board to debate issues surrounding the state's policy of permitting student-athletes to participate in athletic programs with a D- average. The question must be raised: What colleges/universities are admitting Black male student-athletes in particular into the halls of higher education with the D- average they bring from various high schools in South Carolina?

In all honesty I do not expect the state's policy makers to change what should be an embarrassing standard for any high school; however, I am just one man, who is speaking out on the issue!

## GPA and Honest Self-Assessment

Earlier in the book Black male student-athletes were asked to conduct an honest self-assessment to help determine the direction they should consider taking before "putting all their eggs in the one basket" of becoming a professional athlete. As mentioned previously there are a plethora of careers and industries where one could become a "pro" outside of professional sports. For the Black male student-athletes who may be interested in exploring alternative careers and industries outside of professional sports, I would encourage them to consider and investigate the fields of Science, Technology, Engineering, and Mathematics, commonly referred to as the S.T.E.M. courses/curricula/major areas of interest. Be assured that those majoring in one or more of the STEM fields should be able to find meaningful careers in and out of the sports industry. It is not my intent to discourage student-athletes from performing at the professional level. However, as stated previously, the likelihood of making a living in professional sports is dismal at best (see chapter four's statistical probabilities of going pro).

# A Special Message for High School Student-Athletes

If you are a Black male student-athlete attending high school, now is the time for you if you aspire to attend college after graduation, to consider the offerings in this chapter.

Now, if you are struggling academically, you are strongly encouraged to identify your best learning style and have a discussion with your parent(s)/guardian(s), and teachers about this important subject. Kunjufu (2011) argues that by identifying and practicing your best learning style it helps to assure your academic success. Here are five primary learning styles Dr. Kunjufu identified: *Visual Learner, Visual-print, Visual-pictures, Oral/Auditory, and Tactile/Kinesthetic Learners.* To learn more about these learning styles, I encourage you to get a copy of: *Understanding Black Male Learning Styles* (Kunjufu, 2011). Although this book was designed and targeted to those in grades K–12, I assure you that the guiding principles are transferable to college and university-level learning. Assessing and evaluating where you are academically and athletically will be a key to assisting you in your decision making as it pertains to your career development. Think about it this way. If you are 15–25 years old, there is a good likelihood that most of your life is ahead of you! So now is the time to plan how best to make smart choices for your future.

If you have read this far in the book, perhaps this would be a good time to revisit the Black Male Student-Athletes' Self-Assessment Survey (BMSASAS). This time, I encourage you to sit with a family member, guidance counselor, coach, spiritual advisor, or anyone whose judgment you trust and who will be truthful with you as it pertains to your responses to the BMSASAS. In addition, take the time to revisit chapter five and re-read the topics outlined on the community of self; this should provide further self-analysis. These two reviews will hopefully help to motivate you to focus on elevating your grade point average (GPA), which could present you with academic and athletic advantages.

## The Importance of Planning and Resourcefulness

In the author's view, there are two things in life that cannot be substituted: Experience and Preparation!

You may be surprised to know that there are additional tools for learning at your disposal. For example, start seeking out the college student-athletes from your own community and begin questioning them about the experiences, challenges, and triumphs they faced as current or former college or university student-athletes. You might find them located in informal settings such as at local playgrounds, community centers, and gyms. Or you might find them through more formal means, by contacting Black fraternities and high school/college alumni associations, for example. Internet searches will help you locate contact information for the more formal possibilities. By conducting your own research, you will find some valuable information from those who have gone where you have yet to go hopefully to college. You are especially encouraged to speak with current or former Black male student-athletes who dropped out of college before graduating, as well as those who were athletes during their college days and graduated without ever receiving any interest from a professional sports organization, but yet they earned their degrees. If you are intentional in your exploration, be assured that the information you glean from the men in both categories could prove to be invaluable.

As a former student athlete who played basketball at various levels such as high school, U.S. Navy 7th Fleet, and the old semi-pro league known as the Eastern League at the time, I have had several conversations with former NBA players, those who attended college and graduated, and those who dropped out before earning their degrees, and have noticed that their conversations are quite different. In order to protect their anonymity, I've used only their first names.

A short time ago I met with Ron, a former NBA player. We had a heart-to-heart talk about the value of Black male student-athletes earning their college degrees. Ron admitted that he did not earn his degree while attending a Big Ten University several decades ago. Ron spoke about how his NBA career ended because of injury on the court, but he also admitted to sustaining "injuries" off the court as well primarily through his use and abuse of alcohol and drugs. Furthermore, Ron also spoke of his regret for not completing his education while attending the university. When questioned about what his post-NBA career and earning power were like after the NBA checks stopped coming, Ron spoke about how he has bounced from job to job, most of which could be classified as "dead-end jobs." Another interesting aspect of his college career that Ron highlighted was the fact that, his university coach and academic advisor encouraged him to take mostly "easy courses" such as psychology and sociology. Although, both psychology and sociology degrees have merit in society and the education can be used to aid large segments of the population. However, as I probed further, Ron revealed that he was really interested in majoring in business administration or nonprofit community development. His goal back then was to start a non-profit business and provide community development training for the youth of Harlem, New York.

In addition, Ron spoke about how he allowed his ego (see chapter five on the community of self) to dictate his actions or in this case, his non-action related to his not returning to the university where he began his studies or to some other college to complete his degree work. Since Ron was aware that his comments would be highlighted in this book, he implored me to make sure to highlight the need for Black male student-athletes to stay and complete their education. Doing so would provide a plethora of alternatives that could lead to a successful life and career outside of the athletic arena.

Several months later I met with James, another former standout college-athlete when he played basketball for his university. His athletic talents provided him with an opportunity to actually be contacted by a professional sports organization and he was offered a tryout with his hometown team, the New York Knickerbockers. Although James made it to the final cut, he was not offered a professional contract. At this juncture, James surmised that he wanted to be able to provide a good living for himself and his family, so he returned to the university immediately and stayed to earn both his baccalaureate and master's degrees. Today James is a successful entrepreneur.

When we think about their rejections by pro sports organizations, neither man's story could be classified as unique. However, both men stressed the need for Black male student-athletes who are fortunate enough to reach a college/university campus to make earning their degrees a top priority in spite of their athletic prowess.

## Vital Resources

One of the most overlooked resources for student-athletes are found on campus. As stated previously, when you build relationships (network) with professors, student support services departments, athletic administrators, and coaches, you develop a critical component of successful planning during college days and after your college career has concluded. Unfortunately, the tunnel vision that many Black male student-athletes tend to develop, oftentimes early in life, could be part of the cause of so many not earning their degrees, regardless of whether they are contacted by a professional sports organization. Therefore, the value of proper planning can and should not be underestimated. And, for those student-athletes who are still undecided about which direction they would like to pursue, taking advantage of the resources available to them on campus, and within their home communities, and speaking with current and former student-athletes could prove to be an immeasurable method of ensuring a successful career in and outside of the professional sports arena.

Richburg (2013) in his research study on the importance of Black male student-athletes, highlighted the need for Black male student-athletes to develop and strengthen their relationships with the office of student supports services at their high school and later, at their college. Furthermore, Richburg (2013) argued that the need for a liaison to serve between the student-athletes and the student support services department is paramount. When analyzing the results of a survey offered in his research on Black male student athletes in a large urban community Richburg (2013) identified as a primary reason that student support services was such an underused department by Black male student-athletes centered on the belief that student support services providers did not have the student-athlete's best interests at heart. Perceived or real, this was a factor in support services being an underused resource. Furthermore, Kissinger and Miller (2007) argued that many urban based community colleges were limited in their ability to dedicate substantial resources to address the emotional and psychological needs of the general student population, as well as those of Black male student-athletes.

Therefore, those of us who serve in various leadership roles in athletic departments must commit to not having a deleterious effect on Black males in general and Black male student-athletes in particular. As far back as 1984, Harry Edwards, PhD, warned us "as a people, we have the responsibility to learn about the realities of black sports involvement, its liabilities as well as its opportunities and to teach our children to deal with these realities intelligently and constructively" (Edwards, 1984, p. 13).

Another area where a critical analysis must be explored is found in the lack of involvement by many Black male student-athletes in campus activities as mentioned previously. There are many clubs and activities at colleges and universities that offer their students opportunities to grow and develop outside of their participation in athletic events. On-campus fraternities, clubs, and organizations offer Black male student-athlete's opportunities to engage in various activities, such as community service, interfaith ministry, robotics competitions, theatrical productions, to name a few. The student activities department usually has at least one person who serves as a student coordinator to guide interested persons to areas where their growth and development can be enhanced as young education seeking adults. Furthermore, Black male student-athletes can and perhaps should establish (or join) an organization to support the communities surrounding their campus, even if they are not currently living in their communities of birth. Because so many of our young Black males are attracted to athletics, who better to serve as positive role models than those who are currently student-athletes. Although many young Black males are not interested in athletics per se, many do have a need or desire to be mentored and guided, consciously by those who look like them. The sense of familiarity and genuine concern could have a life-long impact on these young brothers.

Many of the Black male student-athletes I have met with and spoken to over the years usually offer reasons for not participating in on-campus activities, such as a lack of time. They often state that between studying, going to practice, attending class, and traveling to games, they say there is not much time to do anything else. Although we should commend those Black male student-athletes who focus on their academic responsibilities with the same vigor that they use to pursue their athletic activities, anyone can be trained in what is commonly referred to as time management. However, the author takes a different view of "time management." He strongly believes that time cannot be managed, simply because we all get the same amount of time daily, weekly, and so on. Furthermore, the author believes that our lives are a series of events, and therefore, our ability to manage the events in our lives can provide time for other interests if we so desire to shift priorities accordingly.

In the next chapter we will explore the role of parents/guardians concerned individuals/groups when it comes to providing guidance and encouragement to Black male student-athletes.

*The state of South Carolina Public Education Department was contacted and asked for a response regarding acceptable student-athlete grade point average to participate in school sponsored athletic events. There was no reply to the author's inquiry.*

**Questions to ponder:**

1. Who are the people in your life whom you trust to help guide you to reach your goals in life?

**Response:**

2. Have you explored the paths of student-athletes you know to glean information on what and how they were successful or not as student-athletes? What did you learn and how does this apply to the interests, dreams, and goals for your life?

**Response:**

3. Are you a student first who happens to be an athlete, or an athlete who happens to be a student?

Note: This question requires in-depth soul-searching.

**Response:**

# CHAPTER SEVEN

# Parental/Guardian Roles

t is apparent that parents, guardians, concerned individuals, and groups would like nothing better than to see than their loved one strive for the goals they have set for themselves, especially if those goals include signing a professional sports contract. However, the first step in this process of goal attainment should be to help ensure that their loved one is receiving a quality education. It is difficult if not impossible for a Black male student-athlete to achieve academic/athletic success when in some states, no meaningful attention is focused on classroom performance. Furthermore, very few if any post-high school institutions of higher education will accept a GPA of D- when considering admission of a student or student-athlete into their freshman class. Unless, of course, academic achievement does not really matter. Sadly, more and more institutions of higher education place emphasis on the revenue that can be generated through their "student"-athletes' participation in sports. This is especially true for the larger conferences in the country. Let us take a look at the "dreamers."

# The Dreamers

Failure to balance earning a degree against their son making a profession-al sports team can create unrealistic expectations for student-athletes and sometimes their families as well. Coupled with their own desires, Black male student-athletes can often feel so much pressure to provide for their families, that a psychological term known as cognitive dissonance becomes an influencing factor. Cognitive dissonance is defined as: "the state of having inconsistent thoughts, beliefs, or attitudes, especially as relating to behavioral decisions and attitude change" (www.Dictionary. com). Moreover, too many parents, guardians, and others have visions of their sons going to college and entering the professional draft classes of primarily basketball or football. For some reason, baseball is not as attrac-tive as it once was for Black male student-athletes. They often dream of the financial security that a professional contract can bring to themselves and their families. Sadly, the statistical realities say otherwise. For exam-ple, less than one-tenth of 1 percent of all student-athletes participating in college/university athletic programs ever receive an inquiry of interest from representatives of professional sports organizations.

The question that must be raised is: Why are the parents, guardians, and others of these Black male student-athletes not more involved in the high school education of their sons? Basically, there are two reasons why parents, guardians, and others do not pay the necessary attention to their son's high school education: 1. Many of the parents and guardians of Black male high school student athletes are often forced to focus on the basics needed to ensure that their families have food, clothing, and shelter; 2. Parents and guardians are not the only ones who can or have developed the "tunnel vision" mentioned previously. Please understand, I am not making blanket statements about the plight of all Black family's economic situation who have student athletes in their homes.

Recently the host/producer of a call-in radio show challenged the leadership of the local school district in my area of the Southeast to come and debate the issue of allowing student-athletes to participate in sports activities with only a D- grade point average. No one in leadership agreed to show up. Is it possible that the leadership of the local school district knows full well that the "quality" of education being received by the local high school student-athletes is woeful? Could it be true that to require or demand better academic performances would somehow expose the leadership's lack of interest in their academic performances? Might such exposure increase the number of inquiries from parents and other concerned community members to begin exploring options to remedy these deficiencies, which could result in removal of some of those in school leadership?

Now is the time for these parents, guardians, and others to accept the fact that going pro will never be more than a fantasy for the vast majority of parents and caregivers of these young men. As a matter of fact, fewer than 2 percent of college student-athletes ever play professional sports at any level for any amount of time (Farmer, 2019). For example, each year when the NFL conducts their annual draft, only 224 of the hundreds of thousands of college players are selected. Unfortunately, that statistic often fails to register with many of the scores of thousands of college student-athletes. This reality is particularly valid for those Black male student-athletes who are singularly focused on the rare chance that they will ever join the ranks of professional athletes. My impressions are consistent with a 2015 NCAA survey, which confirmed that 64 percent of Division I football players believe it is "somewhat likely" that they will become a professional athlete. Here is a fact that we should take into account: only 1 in 4,233 high school players go from high school to college to the pros.

## What about the college degree?

Let us take a look at Black male student-athletes who do not earn their college degree within six years of enrolling at their college or university. Here are some of the typical reasons that Black male student-athletes do not earn their college degrees: 1. Many in this group find themselves no longer eligible to participate in their sport(s); 2. For those who do not receive "full scholarships" they run out of money for college or declare themselves eligible for the professional draft, but they do not get drafted. (This happens especially to football players). The National Basketball Association uses a different format for high school and college players. There are no eligibility restrictions where the NBA is concerned. However, the end game is usually the same.

More on these troubling statistics is provided by Harper (2016). Although in this particular study Dr. Harper's focus was on the Power Five Division I colleges and universities specifically, his musings are applicable and valid for colleges and universities across the United States. Although the major college conferences that generate the most annual revenue are usually favored. It is important to keep in mind, Black male student-athletes who are enrolled in Power Five Division I colleges and universities have access to the very best facilities, medical care, and "booster" organizations, some of which rival or exceed support facilities and services offered by some National Football League teams. Accordingly, only 55 percent of the Black male student-athletes attending these schools graduate within six years after enrollment. The 55 percent graduation rate is significantly lower than the 60 percent of all Black undergraduate men, 69.3 percent of all student-athletes, and 76.3 percent of all undergraduate students who graduated within that six-year time frame (Harper, 2016).

Unfortunately, when the realities set in for most college athletes, they find themselves at the proverbial finish line without their degree or a professional sports contract. Obviously, this is not the goal. While only one college football player wins the coveted Heisman Trophy each year, a college degree is attainable by every player on every team. More importantly, a college degree enhances a person's ability to position themselves in the workplace to earn a good living for themselves and their families. In addition, there are alternatives to entering the world of work, as is discussed more in chapter nine. Entrepreneurship is another option and having a degree in hand provides a primary or secondary opportunity for going into business for one's self.

# The Role of Parents, Guardians, and Others

It should not be difficult for parents, guardians, and others concerned individuals or supporting organizations to see why the graduation rates are lower for those athletes who attend schools where football and basketball are a priority. A review of a typical schedule will confirm that actually, being a college athlete is a demanding and intense "full-time job!" A recent survey conducted by the NCAA revealed, for example, that playing college football alone requires 43.3 hours per week of practice, training, medical attention where needed, and travel during the season that their sport is being played. Such a schedule leaves very little time for members of this group to attend classes, complete assignments, and prepare for examinations. Furthermore, the website NCAA.org acknowledged in one of its advertisements that there are more than 380,000 student-athletes nation-wide and most of them will go pro in something other than sports. But student-athletes cannot be expected to do these things on their own. They need the support of people at their institutions, from administrators to coaches to faculty, to help make reaching their academic goals just as important, perhaps more important than reaching their goals in a particular sport.

Therefore, the role of parents, guardians, and others is extremely critical to Black male high school student-athletes getting off to a good start academically and athletically. It is important to specify the role of the "others" mentioned throughout this chapter. Having worked with some of the "others," I must caution readers to understand and remain vigilant when it comes to permitting access to their sons. When it comes to guiding their sons, especially those with superb athletic skills, one of the tactics used by many college coaches and scouts is to identify not only family members, but so-called "friends" of the family who could easily influence those young Black male student athletes to attend this school or that school and make promises many of them unkept promises to the athletes and their families. Over the years I have had experiences where a trusted family friend was financially compensated for steering their son to a specific college or university. Unbeknown to the family, to steer student athletes to selected colleges and universities with promises of nice cars, cash in their pockets, and all the girlfriends they can manage. Most deplorable is the promise to give the student-athlete easy courses to enhance their chances of remaining eligible to participate in sports after questionable admission tactics have been deployed in more cases than are commonly known.

Sadly, many of the parents and guardians with whom I have interacted over the years, they really love their sons and want the very best for them. But oftentimes they are shown the "glitter" of what a professional sports contract could provide. However, all that glitters is not gold! Therefore, those of us who truly understand the statistical probabilities know that the chances of their son making it to the professional ranks are a long shot at best. Having seen the downside of what happens when athletically gifted high school Black male student-athletes are not properly guided. The lifetime impact is and can continue to be devastating!

Perhaps you recall, in the Introduction, I provided an example of an incident that happened one day when I entered a McDonald's eatery in Manhattan, New York. The young man who took my order was well-known nationally as an All-American high school basketball star. He attended New York City's Rice High School in Harlem and was terribly mishandled and used by a so-called "friend of the family." Interestingly, at the time Rice High School was one of the premier academic and basketball power schools in New York City, known not only for producing top-notch Division I basketball players, but they were and still are renowned as a first-rate academic high school as well.

Once this dreadful pandemic has subsided, I plan to approach my local high school district's leadership and offer to volunteer as a liaison of sorts to work with and help prepare Black male student-athletes who are interested in attending college. I plan to help prepare them academically as well as athletically to take the next crucial step on their life's journey.

In chapter five of this book Black male student athletes were introduced to the community of self and the critical role it could have in their decision-making processes. In chapter eight, the reading expands on chapter five and is designed to assist the student athlete with developing personal standards or principles by which to conduct their day-to-day lives. These principles could assist Black male student athletes' overall development as a "principled" young man.

**Questions to ponder:**

1. Have you been introduced to and prepared to take pre-college examinations such as the American College Testing (ACT) and/or the Scholastic Aptitude Test (SAT)?

**Response:**

2. Are you aware that there are **free** ACT and SAT preparation exams and preparation mentors throughout the country?

**Response:**

3. Are you willing to seek assistance from a source who is knowledgeable and one whom you trust before signing a letter of intent to enroll in a specific college or university to participate in their sports programs?

**Response:**



4.  What do you plan to do to help your parent(s) /guardian/concerned other person(s) to become more knowledgeable about yours and their expectations as they pertain to attending college as a student-athlete?

**Response:**

# CHAPTER EIGHT

# Spiritual Principles to Live By

Having been developed over the past 85 years, the following principles have proven to improve the lives of those who engage in the daily practice of these principles to the best of their abilities. These principles should be practiced regardless of one's religious or spiritual beliefs.

As the Black male student-athlete grows and develops in his practice of these principles, doing so could help to ensure that the transition from school to the world of work, even if that work leads him to the world of professional sports the practicing these principles helps to ensure his success no matter his life's journey may lead him. A word of caution, do not permit any religious or spiritual beliefs/practices to which you may have adhered to previously, prevent you from considering following these simple guidelines to practical and spiritual freedom for yourself.

## Basics

One of the first steps to take on this recommended road to real freedom is to determine what the term "spirituality" means to you. Not to be confused with the term religion which has been identified as a set of beliefs and "principles" that are practiced by an individual or groups that usually culminate with a God or gods at the core of those beliefs and practices. On the other hand, spirituality has been defined as; the quality of being concerned with the human spirit or soul as opposed to material or physical things.

During my life's journey I have also been exposed to various groups who define religion and spirituality in this manner; Some say that religion is for people who are not trying to go to "hell" and "spirituality" is for people who have already been to "hell!"

You may wonder, what is the connection between sports and spirituality? This concept may seem hard to grasp at first. For example, you don not usually see much evidence of "spirituality" at a football game, with 22 men running around a field chasing a ball and each other, and 50,000 fans shouting and gesticulating at them. Taylor (2002) contends that sports is important because it is one of the most readily available ways of generating the state commonly referred to by athletes as "being in the zone." Being in the zone is a component of dhyana which is defined according to dictionary as a profound meditation which is the penultimate stage of yoga, generally found in the practice of yoga and defined as having full consciousness and self-awareness.

Many Black male student-athletes were raised in environments and homes where the Christian religion was a foundational principle of how to "live right" before God and or Jesus. Perhaps during their youth and adolescent years many Black male athletes paid little if any attention to their grandmothers, who were the primary family members dragging them off to church on Sundays. The resentment and dislike conjured up during those years was enough to turn off many Black male student-athletes from anything to do with organized religion. During those years, spirituality or one's spirit of invisible power may not have been identified as such; nonetheless, all humans have that inner phenomenon readily available when called upon which can drive a person to exist in a "zone" of consciousness. Usually in sports we use other terms like "the will to win" which we loosely translated can be stated as; What's Important Now (W.I.N.).

Great players have the ability, when the game is on the line, to reach deep within themselves to elevate and oftentimes surpass their opponents' "will to win."

This chapter was developed to help athletes better understand that "internal happenings" which propels them to press on when their body sends a signal to the brain that they cannot go any further. Moreover, somehow athletes as much as any other performers realize on some level that finding more "energy" to go on is simply an act of the will or spirit.

## Spiritual Well-being and Athletic Performance

In fact, it's possible to say that depending on your definition of spirituality, the desire to experience spiritual well-being is one reason why sports are such an integral part of society's existence. When one is in the zone, unusual things may happen. Spiritual teachers inform us that psychic and paranormal abilities emerge naturally when an athlete is in higher states of consciousness. For example, when competing hard or being in a zone which is a side effect of spiritual progress, athletes occasionally experience these highs. There are moments when suddenly everything "clicks", and the student-athlete shifts to a higher level of athletic performance and becomes capable of astounding feats. This is an example of our spiritual selves being in tune with not only the physical aspect of existence but is also a time when our spirituality is elevated as well. Such activities can take place even if we do not identify this "happening" as having to do with spiritual awareness.

Perhaps the student-athlete may be wondering: What does all this talk about developing spiritual awareness and practices have to do with their holistic development? Think about this phenomenon called spiritual development and growth that a coach might include in his instructions while he provides guidance to athletes to help improve their performance. To improve performance, the student-athletes must be willing to work to enhance their performance. How does an athlete's performance improve? The athlete must be willing to focus on the lessons the coach is trying to teach. Developing one's spirituality comes with lessons as well. The principles outlined below provide lessons that when practiced daily, help to ensure that a more balanced individual can emerge. Another way of capturing the meaning and essence of the principles outlined in this chapter is to look at them as "doing the right things, for the right reasons" in every area of one's life.

Have you ever noticed that at the peak of a tremendous and victorious performance the blood seems to be pounding in your head, and all of a sudden, things become quiet within you? Taylor (2002) argues that everything seems clearer than ever before, as if great spotlights have been turned on. Taylor (2002) contends that the moment you have the conviction that you are capable of anything, that you have wings! This is an example that your spiritual self is functioning at a much higher level than usual. As you develop the daily habit of practicing some or all the principles presented here, in time it will begin to make more sense and help to guide you to what may be a "new place" in your existence. In other words, you can realize that you can be in a "zone" when not participating in your particular sporting event.

In chapters two and five of this book, you are encouraged to explore yourself internally in order to assist your growth and development beyond the classroom and athletic activities in which you are involved. By revisiting chapter two you will notice that there are no right and wrong ways to conduct this self-assessment. Perhaps you are asking yourself, what do chapters two and five have to do with earning my degree while remaining athletically inclined to reach the professional level of my sport? Because your responses to chapters two and five are so deeply personal, perhaps having a conversation with those whom you trust and respect to tell you the truth as they view it, could turn out to reveal some "blind spots" within you. Many people like to project to the outside world that they are full of confidence, in some cases supremely so. However, ongoing self-assessment and evaluation play a critical role in one's overall development and can reveal nuances of which he may not have been aware or admitted to. For example, as a student-athlete how often has the image you project to both your teammates and opponents been not quite the way you feel inside? Or, what about those occasions when competing in street ball games when you did not feel as confident as you projected? What did you do with those feelings and thoughts? No matter what image one projects outwardly, in order to develop and maintain a balanced existence, it is important to always be true to one's self.

Think about this example. Have you ever submitted an assignment to your professor or taken an examination feeling confident that you have done well on both, only to discover when you receive your grade that you did not perform as well as you thought you would? What are some of the first thoughts and feelings that come to mind? Could you honestly say to yourself that you did your very best, or did you use or look for ways to get around putting in the work necessary to ensure a better outcome? The truth of the matter is, you and only you know where the truth lies. Following the set of principles outlined in this chapter helps to assure you that you have a solid foundation for bringing more balance to your daily life.

## Principle One

**Honesty**: Honorable, sincere, truthful/open, frank, candid/will not lie, cheat, or steal; real/correct/absent of pretense. Do not add to or take away from. Free from fraud or deception, marked by free, forthright, and sincere expression.

**Acceptance:** Enduring, bearing, putting up with patiently and without protest or reaction/belief in the goodness of something.

## Principle Two

**Hope:** Assured and excited anticipation that the desired can and will be achieved. A profound belief that things can and will get better.

## Principle Three

**Faith:** A firm belief in something for which there is no logical, material, or absolute proof. Trust without reservation. Believing, not seeing. Trusting not questioning. Belief in the truth, value, or trustworthiness of an idea or principle. Reliance/allegiance.

## Principle Four

**Courage:** The quality of mind or spirit that allows one to face danger, fear, or difficulties with self-confidence and determination. God-given natural awareness of right and wrong. Acknowledgment of the conscience/self-accusing spirit.

## Principle Five

**Integrity:** Living according to a strict moral code; upright; honest.

## Principle Six

**Willingness:** More than a desire or being agreeable. The actual use of one's willpower to follow through and do something.

## Principle Seven

**Humility:** A clear, honest recognition of who and what I really am, followed by an equal desire and willingness to become what I could be.

## Principle Eight

**Brotherly Love:** Deep affectional feelings and caring as one would for a brother/sister.

**Justice:** Right or reasonable/fair treatment. Treating others as we would like to be treated.

## Principle Nine

**Self-Discipline:** Control or restraint in one's behavior.

## Principle Ten

**Perseverance:** Continuing, despite obstacles or discouragement; keeping at it. Continuing to search and maintain desire to do what is right and just.

**Open-Mindedness:** Being inclined to respect views and beliefs that differ from one's own; ready and willing to favorably receive new and different ideas or opinions of others.

### Principle Eleven

**Spiritual Awareness:** For those who consider and value spiritual concepts and principles. A gift which amounts to a new state of consciousness and being. A product of the spirit or soul as distinguished from the body of material matters.

### Principle Twelve

**Love:** LOVE is an action word. God or Higher Power is Love!
**Service:** Aiding in the benefits to others.

**Questions to ponder:**

1. What thoughts or understandings if any did you have about your spirituality? How might these have changed now that you have read this chapter?

**Response:**

2. Are you able discern that there is a difference between spirituality and religion? In your view, what is the difference?

**Response:**


3.  Are you willing to practice the 12 principles outlined in this chapter and begin monitoring how your life has changed as a result?

**Response:**

# CHAPTER NINE

# Entrepreneurship
# (Doing for Self and Others)

To become an entrepreneur, one must first become familiar with the basics. Entrepreneurship is defined as "the activity of setting up a business or businesses, (and) taking on financial risks in the hope of profiting (www. onlinedictionary.com). In addition, the terms "entrepreneurship" and "entrepreneur" are sometimes used interchangeably. **Entrepreneurship is regarded as an abstraction,** whereas an entrepreneur is regarded as a **tangible person.** The tendency of a person to organize one's own business and run it profitably is regarded as entrepreneurship. In this chapter you will find a series of steps necessary to becoming an entrepreneur.

Becoming an entrepreneur is a challenging proposition, especially when it comes to obtaining start-up capital. Most successful entrepreneurs usually start developing their business on a part-time basis. For example, once you familiarize yourself with the seven start-up steps listed below, your next step is to seek guidance from successful entrepreneurs.

Most are willing to help you and will share information and in some cases their resources, including how to obtain start-up capital. After all, many entrepreneurs provide a service as well as products, so naturally they want you and your family and friends to be among their loyal customers.

In chapter eight you read and hopefully began practicing the 12 principles listed. I encourage you to focus on, review, and internalize Principles One, Five, Six, Nine, and Ten. By using and incorporating the principles in your everyday life, success is sure to follow. Below are the seven start-up steps that successful entrepreneurs use. In addition, there are detailed definitions which could serve as a guide to developing an entrepreneurial business.

## Before You Begin Your Start-Up

**An important point to remember when it comes to starting out as an entrepreneur: If you are working for an employer it's generally best to begin your entrepreneurial journey on a part-time basis.**

As a student-athlete many advisors would recommend the following precautions be taken.

- Wait until you are done with your eligibility before you start a business so you can focus on your sport.

- You won't have any time to create a business while you're a student-athlete.

- You don't have enough experience to own a business while still in school.

- Most student-athletes graduate with no work experience and generally have no way to make income outside of financial aid.

Here is a term that you may not be familiar with, "studentathletepreneur," which simply means a student-athlete who is interested in starting their own business while serving as a student-athlete. On September 30, 2019, California Governor Gavin Newsom signed into law the Fair Play to Pay Act that, effective 2023, will allow student-athletes to profit off their own name, image, and likeness. Although at this juncture, California is the first state to do this and therefore student-athletes are currently prohibited from such pursuits, the NCAA's board of governors voted unanimously to direct each of its divisions to update bylaws and policies to permit students the opportunity to benefit. With monetization opportunities seemingly inevitable at this point, social media is regarded as one of the easiest ways for student-athletes to begin generating revenue as soon as new rules are in place (Dosch, 2020). In the online magazine Business College Sports, Farnsworth (2019) recommends that high school and college student-athletes who are interested in becoming entrepreneurs need to be cognizant of the importance of keeping their priorities straight and keeping it real. If you are a high school student-athlete bear in mind, if you choose to bring folks on social media along for the ride while you navigate life as a high school athlete, you may just carve out a path that is comfortable as you transition to collegiate athletics.

## Special Relevance for Black Male Student-Athletes

One of the challenges for most Black male student-athletes who come from homes or communities where a scarcity exists when it comes to entrepreneurship (business ownership), they must be willing to search out entrepreneurs who have experienced success. As stated previously, several of the Black male student-athletes consulted with and interviewed for this book seem to think that starting their own business and becoming an entrepreneur has limited value. I beg to differ. As with any new venture or idea, having the proper amount of education and correct information is critical to any success that can be achieved, especially in the entrepreneurship industry.

As the title of this chapter indicates, entrepreneurship (doing for self and others) involves the use of spiritual principle number 12, Service:

Aiding in the benefits to others. There is a biblical and spiritual principle, which when paraphrased simply means, when you help others with what you have received, the giver will always have more to give. This means that you will have more for yourself as you give to help others. Within most Black communities you can find community-based resources like churches, mosques, and community-based organizations that could provide a base from which to operate and begin developing a network comprised of those who are willing to help you. Whether you are a new start-up entrepreneurial business or a well-established entrepreneur, the use of informal settings such as small groups of neighbors and fraternity members is a way that Black male student-athletes can begin to develop their business ideas.

Revisiting the chapters presented in this book, especially the chapters on industry of interest (chapter four), grade point averages matter (chapter six), and the community of self (chapter five) could help Black male student-athletes formulate ideas for start-up businesses as entrepreneurs. Since this chapter focuses on doing for self and others, it's important to consider who you are and what makes you get up in the mornings and how these characteristics influence your ability to fulfill your interests. It's also valuable to consider how your start-up business can function within the interconnections between you and others. This is a long-held tradition in Black communities and one that, as mentioned previously, benefits you as well as others.

Earlier in this chapter I spoke about how Black male student-athletes can capitalize on the upcoming law in the state of California set to launch in 2023. For instance, they can begin to capitalize on their name, image, and likeness in order to monetize their ability to generate financial profits for themselves while helping others to do the same. For further clarity, "others" could be family members, classmates, organizations that you may want to support financially and in other ways. Your "others" could also be those who have been placed in your path who could possibly benefit from the products and/or services you could offer as an entrepreneur.

# Get Back on the Block

Of course, if you are a Black male student-athlete enrolled in a college or university that lacks the exposure of some of the bigger schools, the idea of becoming an entrepreneur should have greater appeal for you. Moreover, as has been emphasized, one can become a professional in many industries other than professional sports. One of the best ways to identify opportunities where you could create a start-up business as an entrepreneur is to take an "unofficial survey" of your block, neighborhood, community, or city. Look around and see what products and services are lacking, see which services or products you could provide as a Black male student-athlete entrepreneur. When you make the decision to become a student-athlete entrepreneur, I can assure you that the power that gives you the breath of life, the God or Universal Energy who is known by many names will put people in your path to help you! And when you help others get what they need and want, you can experience and understand the meaning of "The Reciprocal Flow of Abundance" (Richburg, 2016).

Furthermore, it is imperative to keep in mind that you could be appealing to large audiences, especially when marketing yourself and your brand once you have identified the area(s) on which you would like to focus on as a new entrepreneur. If you are like most Black male student-athletes you are more than likely well known in your neighborhood, community, city, state, or nationally. Therefore, you should always be cognizant of your use of content, words and images that could hurt you more than help down the road. Always keep in mind that you want the content about your product/service to appeal to large audiences, and you need your content to be rated as PG-13 as possible. Furthermore, one of the things that could ruin sponsorship and marketing opportunities, and your success as a student-athlete entrepreneur, could be inappropriate content found online on the various social media platforms where you are active.

There are primarily three types of "'hoods" that you should always be aware of and function in:

- The first 'hood' is of course your manhood

- Next comes brotherhood, and

- Third is community-hood

Your success at establishing, maintaining, and reinforcing the connections between these 'hoods' helps to maintain your integrity, authenticity, and your sense of self as a student-athlete entrepreneur.

Another word of caution: student-athletes in general and Black male student-athletes, in particular must have an aura of maturity about them in high school and college. Displaying a proper level maturity could prove to be tough especially when peers have the freedom to do and post anything. After all, you are focusing on creating an alternative to the pros outside of working for a professional sports organization.

## Moving Forward as an Entrepreneur

Below are seven suggested recommendations for further exploration as you consider whether to pursue a career as an entrepreneur. The following provides a brief synopsis of the entrepreneurial process.

## Step 1: Find the right business for you.

Entrepreneurship is a broad term, and you can be an entrepreneur in just about any area. However, you will have to pick a field to work in and a business to start. Start by identifying a business that will not only be successful but is something that you are passionate about. Entrepreneurship is hard work, so you want to focus your attention on something you care about.

## Step 2: Determine if you should get an education and how much further education if any is needed.

In most cases, you do not need to have any type of formal education to be an entrepreneur, but that does not mean you should ignore education entirely. If you want to start a tech company, gain experience in business, computer programming, and marketing could all be valuable tools. Moreover, some industries will likely require some type of formal education, such as owning your own accounting or law firm for example.

## Step 3: Plan your business.

Before you begin to develop your business, you need to have a business plan. A business plan lays out any objectives you have as well as your strategy for achieving those objectives. This plan is important for getting investors on board, as well as for measuring how successful your business is right from the very beginning.

## Step 4: Find your target group/audience.

Not every business appeals to everyone. The age, gender, income, race, and culture of your target group will play a large role in determining where you open your shop, or if you even need to have a physical address for your business. Research which group fits your business model best, and then gear everything to attract that demographic.

## Step 5: Network.

While networking is important in all fields, it is most important for start-up entrepreneurs. Networking is how you meet other people who might have skills and resources you can use in developing your business. You can also find potential investors through networking to help get your business model off the ground. Your network can also support your business once you open, helping send new customers your way.

## Step 6: Sell your idea.

You should be focused on promoting ("selling") your idea before, during, and after you start your business. You may have the best restaurant in the city, but nobody will visit if they do not know it exists. When you engage in promotions, you use tools such as press releases, zoom parties, postcards and emails, launch events, etc., all designed to attract the public, especially your target audience and you can increase their awareness of and interest in your business. Promotional activities involve creativity, they stretch your ability to use your networking and business plan more effectively. Selling your idea can also involve meetings with prospective investors, including banks, where you "pitch" (present persuasively) your business idea to acquire investments of cash, loans, and/or in-kind services (trading/exchanging services or products with other businesses). Steps 3, 4, and 5 above will help tremendously with this step.

## Step 7: Marketing Strategy

In Step 7, the focus is on gathering the data and other information you need to ensure your product or service reaches the most likely and most desired customers. As stated previously, you should always be focused on marketing before, during, and after you start your business. Marketing is tricky, but you should be able to focus your marketing efforts on your target audience by soliciting help from those who have had success as entrepreneurs. For example, millennials may be more likely to see an ad on social media than on a billboard downtown.

## Other Important Facts

In addition to following the steps provided here, it is important to determine if you need a business license. Information on business licensing can be provided free of charge by contacting your local county clerk's office. Furthermore, the business license is usually very cost-effective. Generally, the price ranges from $25.00 to $50.00, and when you think about it, that is a small investment considering the success you could have.

Furthermore, it is also very important to gather information on local, county, state, and federal taxes related to owning your business. You can obtain this information free of charge by going online to the local, county, state, and federal websites (just key in business tax responsibilities) in the search window of each of these websites.

Help is also available at no cost via SCORE (www.score.org), an association of thousands of volunteer business mentors. SCORE offers one-on-one counseling, as well as webinars and other information through their website.

You might also obtain answers to entrepreneurial questions via your network, which should include other entrepreneurs who have learned their start-up lessons well and are probably will share what they have learned.

In addition, I highly recommend that you follow the specific "spiritual principles" outlined in chapter eight. If you decide to pursue an entrepreneurial path to help support yourself and others, it is imperative to remember that you have the potential to serve yourself and help others to do the same.

## A True Story

Several years ago, a young man was sent to me when I served as a criminal court administrator before entering my retirement from local government in 2015 in my home state of New York. This young man was sent to me for general counseling, to protect his anonymity I will call him Rasheed. Rasheed had recently been released from prison after serving four years for drug dealing. Although he was only 24 years old, and at one point had been a promising athlete, he also was a twice-convicted felon.

During one of our counseling sessions, I asked Rasheed if he ever thought of going into business for himself as an entrepreneur. It is important to know that while he was limited from going into certain types of businesses, Rasheed's felony conviction could not prevent him from going into business for himself. I suggested that he start in his community and identify a service or product that could serve his community. As we worked to identify a business, Rasheed spoke about the many senior citizens who lived in his community. Many were disabled to the point where it was difficult for them to do things like going shopping and attending to other essential needs. It was at that point that Rasheed developed an idea to monetize his efforts while serving the needs of the senior citizens in his community. He decided he would provide a grocery pick-up and delivery business service for those seniors. Using the seven principles for developing a business listed above, we were able to go to the local government clerk's office and pay the $35.00 for a business license and just like that, Rasheed was a legitimate business owner.

Before moving from New York to South Carolina in 2015, I spoke with Rasheed and he confirmed that his business had grown to the point where he had hired seven workers who had returned home from prison like he once did. The last time I checked on Rasheed to see how he was doing, he had purchased four vans and employed drivers, all men and women returning to the community from prison.

This true story is provided to hopefully help you become inspired to give serious consideration to becoming an entrepreneur. Now, if a young man like Rasheed who at 24 years old was already a twice-convicted felon could have the success he is having, the sky is the limit for Black male student-athletes like yourself who are already in an environment of learning by attending college or high school!

If you would like assistance with becoming an entrepreneur feel free to contact Dr. Charles Richburg, he can be reached at www.richburgcs. net or call (914) 275-6370.

## Questions to ponder:

1.  Have you ever given serious consideration to going into business for yourself?

**Response:**

2.  If your answer to the above is yes, what steps have you taken to make your idea a reality? If not, why not?

**Response:**

3.  Has the fear of ignorance, fear of failure, or not knowing how to start a business stopped you from pursuing your idea(s)?

**Response:**

# CHAPTER TEN

# Black Male Student-Athletes Capitalizing on COVID-19: A Blessing in Disguise?

B y now the entire country, indeed, the world has experienced the devastation caused by the coronavirus pandemic. At this writing more than 450,000 lives have been lost in America alone. It appears that no segment of society has escaped this deadly virus, which brings me to the topic for this chapter.

The enthusiasm for college sports in general and football in particular has never been higher, despite the tsunami type of attack in which the virus is moving. Since I reside in the southeastern United States, I can attest to the fact that supporters of college football games being played during the 2020 season argue against any deleterious effects of COVID-19 on the players, 75–80 percent of whom are Black males representing the country's Power Five Conferences. The attention of public and private colleges and universities is focused on the estimated $400,000,000.00 that is in jeopardy of being lost if the Big Five Conferences season was cancelled (Cole, 2020).

If you have been in this predicament of having to decide whether to participate in a contact sport such as football or basketball during this pandemic, I hope you stepped back, took a deep breath, and weighed the odds before making your decision to participate during the 2020 football season. Wisdom dictates that you should have consulted with family members and friends who could have perhaps brought some objectivity to your plight. (Please see chapter seven on the ongoing role of parents/guardians/concerned others.) The strategy for deciding to participate is not confined to Division I schools for Black male student-athletes alone. If you are enrolled in a Division II or III school, the same decision-making principles mentioned previously should be applied.

The debate over whether to proceed or not with the fall 2020 football and basketball seasons has been fierce. None other than Nicholas Saban Jr., head football coach at the University of Alabama at Tuscaloosa led the charge in arguing that the fall 2020 season should proceed as scheduled. Saban's reaction to rumors that the season should be cancelled pushed back with such comments as: "The players are safer at school with me at the University of Alabama, rather than 'running around at home'" (Fox News, August 10, 2020). How presumptuous of him to think that he can "protect" his players from an airborne virus that has infiltrated every industry and state in the country. A different viewpoint posited by Eddie R. Cole, Ph.D. an associate professor of higher education and organizational change at the University of California at Los Angeles (UCLA), who made the following assertion: college and university presidents, athletic directors, and some coaches are torn between going forward with their football season despite the warnings from health care professionals and infectious disease specialists (Cole, 2020).

As an educator I view this pandemic as a "blessing in disguise" for some, especially those Black male student-athletes who may be taking a more realistic view of themselves and their "real" talent level when it comes to having an opportunity to turn pro. However, if you truly believe that you are properly equipped to make it in professional sports,

I encourage you to "go for it!" I will add this caveat for consideration, many people in general are challenged when it comes to conducting an honest and thorough assessment of themselves and the need for such an assessment is a required endeavor and should not be optional, especially for Black male student athletes at the college/university level. Many student athletes tend to either overvalue or undervalue themselves and their capabilities.

If you have been in the fortunate or unfortunate position of not being able to compete this season because of the current pandemic, this downtime could perhaps be best spent focusing on your academic goals and responsibilities. By graduating on time, you could provide a safety net of sorts for yourself, even if you think or know that you will be contacted by a professional sports organization.

It is important to understand that I am not unsympathetic toward those who depend on college sports for their livelihood, whole or partial, such as stadium refreshment vendors for example. However, they too will have to decide that, if college sports in their area were to go forward without the Covid-19 restrictions in place during the 2020-2021 seasons, would they feel safe enough to provide food and drink and other amenities to those being entertained in various stadiums and risk becoming infected with the COVID-19 virus. Even if preventive measures such as social distancing, wearing masks, and regular hand washing are somewhat successfully practiced, there is still a risk of infection. And there is no guarantee of contracting a mild case of coronavirus being spread. At this writing, the virus has yet to be contained and vaccinations are still limited in their administration nationwide.

Amid a public health crisis that affects Black male student-athletes disproportionately, college leaders, athletic directors, and some coaches are prioritizing institutional profit over Black lives. Moreover, Black male student-athletes are becoming figurative lab mice as the question of in-person classes is being considered (Cole, 2020).

# The State of Mental Health

In addition to what the general student population is dealing with as it pertains to the COVID-19 pandemic, Black male student-athletes are also faced with issues surrounding the state of their mental health. According to Harper (2016), since Black male student-athletes make up 56 percent of college football teams and 61 percent of men's basketball teams there needs to be special interest paid to members of these groups. Recently, the NCAA conducted a student-athlete COVID-19 Well-Being Survey with over 37,000 participants (Loring, 2020). The results of the survey found that the majority of all student-athletes reported experiencing high rates of mental distress since the pandemic began officially in the U.S. in January 2020. Over a third reported experiencing sleep difficulties, more than a quarter reported feeling sadness and a sense of loss, and 1 in 12 reported feeling so depressed it has been difficult to function constantly or practically every day. Cole (2020) argues that since Black male student-athletes comprise 56 percent of college football players and 61 percent of the men basketball players, the fact that some colleges and universities have made attempts to continue with their seasons being influenced, no doubt by mounting financial losses which could be in the hundreds of millions of dollars indicates that Black male student-athletes' mental health condition is being totally ignored.

Moreover, I contend that both Black and White student-athletes are looking to coaches as their primary source for information on the pandemic, their training, and their mental health state. However, when it comes to Black male student-athletes, it is suspected that many of them may be somewhat hesitant to approach their coaches and discuss their feelings of uneasiness as it pertains to their mental health for fear that doing so could jeopardize their athletic careers.

As college students return to school remotely, in-person, or in a blended format, so do college athletes. But just because class is in session does not mean every school agrees about whether football and basketball players will have a full, uninterrupted season this year. These institutions have quickly learned that containing COVID-19 on campus can be next to impossible, especially as the rate of infection among college-age people spiked over the last six months of 2020 (Centers for Disease Control, 2021). And the decision to bring back college football especially affects Black male student-athletes, who make up a disproportionate share of players. As a matter of fact, one Black male student-athlete currently on Clemson University's nationally ranked football team, shared the following with me in confidence, he believed that the coaches saw the handwriting on the wall.

When asked what effect that may have on Black male student athletes' returning to play, one Southeastern Conference (SEC) representative said it was following the advice of its own medical task force. The SEC's health experts contends that they have guided the schools in their conference through each stage of preparation for the safe return of athletic activity. Together with the medical staffs embedded within their athletics department's programs, the SEC's health experts say that they continue to monitor developments around the virus and their plans have evolved as they continue to meet the health needs of their student-athletes.

## The 2020 Season and Its Impact on Mental Health

Interestingly, while many campuses remained closed during much of the 2020 school year, the college football season, though shortened, went forward. At times, some games were cancelled when players (or coaches and staff) tested positive for the Covid-19 virus. In addition, stadium attendance was restricted, though not stopped completely. Overall, with a definite eye on garnering as much revenue as possible from advertisements and other support components, college football continued all the way to its conference and national championships rounds of play. High school football had a shorten schedule as well, even though a number of COVID-19 related risks and tragedies occurred during the 2020 season. Two 14-year-olds playing for football teams in Georgia and Mississippi contracted COVID-19 and subsequently suffered serious heart and lung conditions (Kearns, Bachynski, and Caplan, 2020). And several football coaches died from COVID-19 complications, including five head football coaches in Georgia, a coach in Mississippi, and coaches in South Carolina and Arizona, among others (Kearns, Bachynski, and Caplan, 2020).

In spite of the precautions, issues related to student athletes' mental health persists. For those Black male student-athletes who do not have the "luxury" of playing in the nation's top football programs, I encourage them to seek out independent counselors, mental health counseling professionals, and mentors rather than relying solely on the advice received from their college or university athletic administrators and coaches as it pertains to the impact of COVID-19 on their mental health. I am not suggesting that all athletic administrators and coaches lack the desire to Black male student-athlete's best interests at heart. However, the fact that they could have conflicting motives could possibly skew the advice given by those in athletic leadership positions. A leading physician and clinical assistant professor of medicine and infectious disease at New York University's School of Medicine, stated that, even though student athletes might have developed healthier, stronger baselines than the average person, they too can suffer the same consequences as those with pre-existing conditions and who are otherwise healthy people. I urge that student-athletes should have a trusted counselor or mental health professional to talk to about their coping difficulties.

According to the sports business program director at Washington University in St. Louis, Missouri, many colleges and universities are already starting to see schools cutting staff and cutting sports programs to offset financial and reputational losses. Furthermore, the financial losses for each school can vary depending on how they calculate their books and determine what is a loss and what isn't. For example, in the Power Five Conferences which are comprised of 65 schools, the financial losses could total approximately 400 million dollars. Moreover, some individual schools in the Power Five Conference could take a $100 million dollar hit.

Although the mental health state of Black male student-athletes should be of uppermost concern in all our minds and as critical as mental health is in these young men's lives, the need for stable mental health evaluations extends beyond the playing field or court for these young men. As indicated in the chapter's title, is it possible that in some ways not having responsibilities associated with athletic participation could be a "blessing in disguise?" As stated previously in this chapter, many student-athletes both Black and White are displaying signs that not being able to participate fully in their particular sport is taking its toll on them psychologically and emotionally. For this and many other reasons, not being able to participate fully in team sports is an ideal time for those who counsel and mentor Black male student-athletes to discuss how they are really feeling and thinking, now that they have had some downtime from their usual training routines and game schedule.

Basically, the question to pose is: "Are they students who happen to be athletes, or are they athletes who happen to be students?"

In a recent study by the Center for Sport Psychology and Performance Excellence at the University of North Texas (July 2020), results showed that only 2 percent of Black male student-athletes have sought out assistance provided by counselors, mental health professionals, medical professionals, and sports psychologists. Interestingly, a small but sizable number of the Black male student-athletes scored at the highest levels in the study, indicating severe impairment in terms of depressive symptoms, psychological distress, and dissatisfaction with life. Moreover, even more fell into the moderate or subclinical level on these same measures. In addition, relatively few athletes reported having no symptoms or experiencing no distress.

## What about academics?

Another area of concern to explore is related to how many Black male student-athletes will or have dropped out of school because of their inability to participate fully in athletic events. Despite the devastation caused by this pandemic, Black male student-athletes have had an opportunity to use their downtime to delve deeper into their studies and perhaps shift their focus from the field or court to the classroom. Regardless of the revised education models that were offered in 2020 and 2021, with many colleges and universities using various course formats such as remote learning, blended, and limited classroom teaching and learning, Black male student-athletes should take advantage of opportunities to improve their grade point averages to help ensure that they can graduate on time. In today's academic environments students are considered successful if they can manage to graduate with a four-year degree (baccalaureate), which traditionally takes four years to complete and has now been expanded to six years. Surely those Black male student-athletes who intend to earn their degrees within the allotted time frame can now think more about or rethink their options, when it comes to searching out alternatives to becoming a professional athlete. They can consider themselves as successful students on their way to a profession outside of sports.

## Final Thoughts

Writing this book was a labor of love for me, providing me with the opportunity to pursue a long-held passion for working with and helping to guide Black males in general, and Black male student-athletes in particular. In the introduction of this book, I shared selected portions from my childhood in the segregated South in the 1950s to the present. One of the lessons I learned was the importance of having proper guidance in life. Furthermore, another goal for writing this book was to ignite the thought processes of Black male student-athletes as it pertains to their clear understanding that there is a plethora of ways to become a pro-outside of playing professional sports to make a good living for themselves and their loved ones. To those who have a measure of influence on Black male student-athletes, it is imperative that you help them to realize and understand that if they do not reach their goal of becoming a professional athlete, it does not mean that they are a failure. Reiterate the fact that they have been fortunate to have an opportunity to earn their degree and to reach a college campus in the first place. This is especially true when you consider that the number of Black males incarcerated in various prisons and jails throughout the United States, compared to the number of Black males in college is atrocious.

As stated previously, it is important to remember that there are two things in life that cannot be substituted: experience and preparation. Therefore, having an opportunity to obtain a college education is immeasurable. As an athlete it does not matter how skilled you may be, to date no athlete has been able to defeat Father Time! An athletic career is time limited, but an education is a lifetime gift when used properly.

Finally, if you feel that you need or want to have further professional career guidance based on the information provided in this book, feel free to contact the author, Dr. Charles W. Richburg, III, at www.richburgcs. net or call (914) 275-6370.

# REFERENCES

Akbar, N. (1985). *The Community of Self.* Tallahassee, FL: Mind Productions & Associates, Inc.

Axson, S. (2020). "College Football Means Big Money. Black Athletes Stand at the Intersection of Risk and Profit." NBC News. https://www.nbcnews.com/news/nbcblk/college-sports-mean-big-money-black-athletes-stand-intersection-risk-n1238450.

Centers for Disease Control, 2021. Retrieved from https://www.cdc.gov/ on November 15, 2020.

Center for Sport Psychology and Performance Excellence (July 8, 2020). COVID – Executive Summary. Retrieved on January 15, 2021 from: covid_executive_summary.final2.july8.2020.pdf (unt.edu)

Cole, E. R. (July 28, 2020). "Playing College Football in 2020 Would Continue to Devalue Black Lives." *The Washington Post.* Retrieved from: https://www.washingtonpost.com/outlook/2020/07/28/playing-college-football-

Cooper, J. N. (2019). *From Exploitation Back to Empowerment: Black Male Holistic (Under) Development Through Sport and (Mis) Education.* New York: Peter Lang Publishing, Inc.

Dictionary.com. Retrieved on Jan. 9, 2021 from https://dictionary.com

Edwards, H. (1984). "The Black 'Dumb Jock': An American Sports Tragedy." *College Board Review,* no. 131, 8–13. ERIC Number: EJ303001

"Entrepreneur." Dictionary.com. Retrieved on January 13, 2021 from: https://dictionary.com

Farmer, A. (2020). "Let's Get Real with College Athletes about Their Chances of Going Pro." The Conversation. Retrieved on Jan. 8, 2021 from: https//Google.com.

Harper, S. (2014). "Black Men as College Athletes: The Real Win-Loss Record." *Chronicle of Higher Education.* Retrieved on Jan. 20, 2014 from: https://www.chronicle.com/article/Black-Men-as-College-Athletes-/144095

Harper, S. (2016). *Black Male Student-Athletes and Racial Inequities in NCAA Division I College Sports.* Philadelphia: University of Pennsylvania Press. Retrieved from: https://nepc.colorado.edu/sites/default/files/publications/Harper_Sports_2016.pdf

Harrison, L., Jr., Bimper, A. Y., Jr., Smith, M. P., & Logan, A. D. (2017). "The Mis-education of the African American Student-Athlete." *Kinesiology Review,* 6(1), 60–69.

Dosch, K. (2020). "How Student Athletes Can Prepare to Become Entrepreneurs." *Entrepreneur.* Retrieved on Jan. 13, 2021 from: https://www.entrepreneur.com/article/343870

Kearns, L., Bachynski, K., & Caplan, A. L. (Nov. 26, 2020). "Add Covid-related Myocarditis, Mechanical Ventilation, and Death to This Year's Football Risks." STAT. Covid-caused health problems, deaths join football-related injuries - STAT (statnews.com). Accessed 1/30/2021.

Kissinger, D. B., & Miller, M. T. (2007). "Profile and Identity of Community College Student Athletes. *Community College Enterprise,* 13(2), 51–60.

Kunjufu, J. (2011). *Understanding Black Males Learning Styles.* Chicago, IL: African American Images.

Leonard, W. M., & Reyman, J. E. (1988). "The Odds of Attaining Professional Athlete Status: Refining the Computations." *Sociology of Sport Journal,* 5(2), 162–169.

Loring, A. (July 2020). "The Impact of COVID-19 on Student Athlete's Mental Health." KXXV-ABC News. Retrieved on July 30, 2020 from: https://www.kxxv.com/news/coronavirus/the-impact-of-covid-19-on-student-athletes-mental-health

"Professional" (2020). Merriam-Webster.com. Retrieved from: https://www.merriam-webster.com/dictionary/professional

Richburg, C. W. III (2013). "An Examination of Community College Black Male Student-Athletes' Perceptions of Student Support Services and Identifying Methods for Improving Service Delivery." *Education Doctoral.* https://fisherpub.sjfc.edu/education_etd/167

Rhoden, W. C. (2006). *40 Million Dollar Slaves: The Rise, Fall, and Redemption of the Black Athlete.* New York, NY: Crown Publishing Group.

Saban, N. (August 10, 2020). "Should the 2020 College Football Season Be Cancelled?" Fox News.

Taylor, S. (Spring 2002). "Spirituality: The Hidden Side of Sport." *New Renaissance.*

Volume 11, No. 1, Issue 36. Retrieved from: http://www.ru.org/index.php/sport/30-spirituality-the-hidden-side-of-sports

U.S. Census Bureau (2017). Population Estimates. Retrieved from https://www.census.gov/quickfacts/fact/table/US/PST045217

# ABOUT THE AUTHOR

Dr. Charles Richburg, III is founder and president of Richburg Career Services, LLC. RCS, LLC is an organization designed to provide career guidance to current/former college-/university-level Black male student-athletes and non-athletic Black males and help them build rewarding careers, including developing as entrepreneurs (business owners).

For the past 10 years Dr. Richburg has served as an associate professor of business, providing instruction to undergraduate and graduate students. In addition, he serves as a consultant for not-for-profit and for-profit businesses. Dr. Richburg also consults on grant writing, community and organizational development, career guidance, and a host of other services, all designed to support those serving in areas to help others. There is an old adage that states: "To whom much is given, much is expected!" Wherever you may be in life, there are always those whom you can help!

Dr. Richburg earned his Doctor of Education degree from Saint John Fisher College in Rochester, New York. He resides in the southeastern United States with his lovely wife, the Reverend Judith Richburg.

Feel free to contact Dr. Richburg www.richburgcs.net or call (914) 275-6370.